# I FIND NO
## *Fault*

---

*The Liberating Power of Forgiveness*

---

# LINDA MARKOWITZ
### *with Ray Ciaramaglia*

# I Find No Fault
## © Linda Markowitz 2020

ISBN: 978-0-578-63453-1
Publisher: Linda Markowitz Ministries

PO Box 1899 ~ Apopka, FL 32704 ~ LindaMarkowitz.com

# Dedication

I dedicate this book to Jesus Christ,
the only One worthy.
Without Him and His extravagant grace,
this story would be impossible.

# Table of Contents

# Foreword

Prepare yourself to be captivated by one of the most faith-riveting books you have ever read. Prepare yourself to become literally embedded in the highest dimension of forgiveness this side of heaven. Prepare yourself to be immersed in a tangible experience of exceptional love that knows no bounds, transforms the mind's perspective of purpose, and catapults you into the model of destiny-driven success.

Linda is transparent in how she shares life; her own life, the life of her daughter, the life of the man who killed her daughter, and the supreme sacrifice of forgiveness that ultimately brought this man into the throes of the depth of forgiveness that literally collapsed his prison walls and set him free.

This book deals with how the deepest of emotions collided with Linda's reasonable faith. You will learn about the power of forgiveness and restoration from God's perspective.

Prepare yourself to begin reading this book only to discover that you can't put it down; not because of how it's crafted, but because of what it teaches. Linda, through tragedy, has mastered the essence of forgiveness that liberates the soul, defines what obedience with intent can produce, and traverses the path of victory that is the result of a forgiving heart.

Prepare yourself to become completely and totally transformed in the miraculous, marvelous, multi-faceted story of triumph over tragedy. Come away with no regrets that you've just spent time in the pages of a book worth reading, a road worth traveling, and a path worth taking.

*Dr. Clarice Fluitt*
*Life Coach, Motivational Speaker,*
*Author, Television Personality, and*
*Founder of Clarice Fluitt Ministries*

# The Grace to Forgive

Years after receiving saving grace that ushered me into the family of God, I met another aspect of God's extravagant grace; the grace that forgives. I met in a tangible way the grace that is the very essence of who God is. That grace came with an impartation of God's might and it strengthened and empowered me in the most difficult situation of my life. It caused Philippians 4:13 to take on a whole new meaning for me. I can do all things through Christ which strengthened me.

The word 'grace' is found more than 150 times in the New Testament and, prior to actually encountering a tangible manifestation of grace, I would have told you that I knew most of those verses and had a good understanding of the power of that word. Though I had sung the song, 'Amazing Grace' countless times, I truly knew very little about the abounding and extravagant grace of God. Grace has many facets and in each one there is an enabling power. The power of the forgiving grace of God brings peace and liberty. We each receive that power when we accept Jesus as our Lord and Savior. We receive it in an even greater measure when we give that same forgiveness to another.

God gives His grace to whosoever will receive it, and He gives more grace to those who will humble themselves and agree with Him and His will (James 4:6).

I received a greater measure of grace when I humbled myself to God and said 'yes' to what I thought at the time was an unreasonable and impossible request. I now know that the definition of humility is absolute dependence upon God. Humility draws God to our side and He came to me in a marvelous way when I yielded to Him. He gave me more grace than I had ever experienced before when I agreed with Him and His will. This book is the story of my agonizing decision to trust God when He asked me to do what I thought was surely impossible and the outcome of my obedience.

I am a grateful recipient of the power of grace that turns death into life, cursing into blessings. I can boldly and confidently say that whatever you face, God's grace is more than sufficient. I trust that the following pages will bless and encourage you and give you strength to reach for greater grace.

# Linda's Story

# CHAPTER ONE

# The Early Years

I married my first love, Max, when I was only 16 years old. He was an attractive sailor that I had met when he was home on his last leave before being discharged from the Navy. I was captivated with him from the first time I saw him. He was older and seemed so grown-up. We had our first child, a daughter we named Marci, when I was 17. She was a healthy and happy baby and I loved being a mom. She was full of energy and filled our household with joy.

Marci was two and a half years old when on a bitter cold Indiana morning two days after Christmas, I was awakened shortly before dawn in labor with our second child. Delivering Marci, had been relatively quick. Despite being a 9-pound 4-ounce butt-first breach, Marci was born in less than six hours of labor. I shouldn't have been surprised that this smaller and normally positioned baby would come quickly, too.

Max worked the night shift and had only been in bed about two hours. Although I knew I was in labor, I decided to let him sleep as long as possible, making sure that my labor pains were progressing before waking him. I lay on the couch, walked the floor, and sat at the kitchen table trying to get comfortable. At about 8:00 a.m. I finally woke Max and told him it was time. He got up and began to diligently implement all of our well-made plans. He called my sister, Charlotte, who lived about 10 miles away, to come and stay with Marci so he could take me to the hospital. He then shaved, showered and got dressed while we waited for my sister to arrive.

In less than 20 minutes, it was very clear to me that our baby was coming. We certainly couldn't leave Marci, and I was in no condition to wake and get her bundled up to go with us so I simply resolved that I would deliver this baby at home. I lay down on the kitchen floor, intending to give birth.

I would have been content to have the baby in our kitchen, but just as I began to push, Charlotte came through the back door and she and Max insisted on getting me to the car. That was no small feat, but they succeeded and carried me to our 1967 Chevelle. The car had a bench front seat and I lay in the front, putting my head in Max's lap. He drove as if he were trying to qualify for a position in the Indianapolis 500 race, but that just wasn't fast enough. We lived several miles from the hospital. We had only driven about 3 miles from the house when our 8-pound, 13-ounce baby girl arrived in the front seat of our car. It was just about the time the doctor's office was scheduled to open and we were closer to his office than we were to the hospital so Max drove me directly to my doctor. I was told later by the staff at the office that Max ran in the front door loudly declaring that he had an emergency. When they asked him what the emergency was, he responded, "It's another girl!" I think he was somewhat in shock.

The doctor came out to the parking lot and cut the baby's cord, bundled her up in disposable paper sheets, and handed her to me. His staff called an ambulance to take us to the hospital. I remember being freezing cold in that ambulance but enjoying the warmth of my newborn child on my chest. She was no longer crying and I could hear her breathe. It was a new beginning. A new life had come into the world. She didn't make a very traditional arrival, but nonetheless, she was finally here and I was so happy. We named her Michele.

At the hospital, nurses took Michele and me to the emergency room to await the arrival of my doctor. He and my husband were following the ambulance in their cars. After my immediate needs were attended to in the ER, I was admitted to a room and the nursery attendants brought Michele to me to have her first feeding. Her face was pink and round and she didn't have a single hair on her head; but she was so beautiful to me. She looked like her father. Those moments alone with her were dear to me. I checked all her fingers and toes and snuggled her close to me. I did not know then that those precious moments would be my last with her for four days. I had contracted the Hong Kong flu and by that evening the symptoms were evident. I was moved to a private room; the hospital staff separated me from everyone, including my new daughter. Because Michele was not born in the hospital, she was given a private room, too, one away from the other newborns. She had very little human interaction in her first four days, just basic care and feeding, and had no contact with me. Her beginning was lonely; she was isolated and alone in a strange new world.

I recovered enough from the flu that the hospital discharged both of us on day five after Michele's birth. I was still weak and needed rest but I had a newborn and her very active two and a half-year-old sister at home, and I had no help. Max had to go back to work on our second day home from the hospital so rest wasn't a priority on my schedule.

Michele's early weeks and months were chaotic at best. She was a restless child and required far more attention than her sister did at the same age. She rarely slept more than two hours at a time and was a fussy eater. She was born with club feet and we began treatment for that when she was six months old. Correcting that condition required a series of braces and special shoes that delayed her ability to walk until she was nearly 16 months old. After her first birthday, it became apparent that she was continually frustrated because she couldn't run and play the way her sister did. That frustration soon began to express itself as anger and Michele became an angry child with a short fuse. When she became agitated, she could rarely be calmed or convinced to go in another direction. Anger began to be etched into her personality and I was so young, only 20 years old, and totally unequipped to help her change.

Once the special braces came off and Michele was able to walk and run, I hoped to see a significant change in her behavior, but that never came. I was a stay-at-home mother at that time and really concentrated on giving her extra time and attention in hopes that would change the course she was on, but nothing I did seemed to have any lasting results. By the time she was three years old, Michele was always angry. Her father said he sensed that she was determined to self-destruct but we didn't know where to turn for help. He had changed jobs and was now an over-the-road truck driver and was gone more than he was home. I was left to rear the girls, however I could, and that was poor at best.

# CHAPTER TWO

# A Tumultuous Interruption

M ax and I divorced after only eight years of marriage; the girls were seven and five years old at the time. The separation and divorce brought incalculable sorrow and confusion that seemed unending. It was an excruciatingly painful situation for all of us, but particularly painful for our youngest daughter, Michele.

I didn't initiate the divorce, but was definitely a willing partner in it. In only a few short months after the divorce was final, I began to deeply regret my participation in ending my marriage and escorting my sweet and vulnerable daughters into a living hell. Over the years I have said more times than I can count that, if I had known the devastating affects the divorce would have on my innocent children, I would have done anything to make that marriage work. I tried on more than one occasion to reconcile with my ex-husband but his heart was cold and his pride too rigid to bend. There was no going back and the girls and I had no alternative but to go on, deeply wounded and alone.

I was not saved at the time of the divorce and did the only thing I knew to do; I jumped into survivor mode and started looking in all the wrong places for anyone or anything that could deliver us from the dark abyss that seemed to devour us. My oldest daughter, Marci, appeared to be a little more resilient than her younger sister, but they both ached for the loss of their father and I hurt with them, and for them.

Divorce was not in the script I had written for my life but was now my reality. About a year after the divorce I moved to a new county in the same state, several miles away from everything I knew to be familiar. I found a job at an insurance company, put the girls in public school and attempted to get some normalcy back into our lives. I was still running my life in survivor mode and all of us were existing, but not truly living.

The divorce caused each of us to become different people, and not in a good way. We were broken, fragmented and desperately lost. Marci soon began to exhibit very aggressive and rebellious behavior that had never been present before. She trusted no one and became very defensive. I watched her entire personality change. Looking back with the wisdom time brings I can see that she somewhat mirrored me and had jumped into survivor mode, trying to find something solid to hang onto for some sense of stability in a life that seemed to be spinning out of control. She was doing all she knew to do to find peace and somehow morphed into a rather grown-up but distorted state of defiance and independence.

Michele reacted very differently. She began to withdraw and became needy, clingy and afraid. She had nightmares and would often cry uncontrollably for no apparent reason. I would sometimes awaken in the morning to find her at the foot of my bed holding on to my feet. She never wanted me to leave, and getting out the door every morning was an ordeal.

Rearing two daughters as a single mom was somewhat a blur for me. I was not only very young; I didn't know the Lord or have any relationship with Him and was clueless on how to be a mother. My own mother died before my sixth birthday and, except for a very brief period in my very young years, I had not been mothered, and had no role model or anyone in my life to teach me how to rear my own children. Admittedly, I wasn't the best mother. I made a lot of mistakes in rearing my girls, some that brought painful consequences, but one thing is undeniable, I love them both deeply and unconditionally. Mothers have a bond with their children that no one else has. That bond is God-given and irrefutable. I see my children as gifts from God and they are very dear to me.

Shortly before our move, I had met and was dating the first of what ultimately became several new men in my life. Thankfully, this man was kind and very helpful. He brought a sense of desperately needed stability and peace to our shattered lives. He was a single father rearing five children alone and was compassionate about my circumstances and extremely good to me and my daughters. We lived separately but, in a sweetly odd sort of way, became a blended family and I began to find my footing again.

Weeks turned into months, and months into years. My first relationship ended for reasons which I take full responsibility, and I once again became obsessed with finding a better life. The girls' father rarely visited and they were deeply hurt by what appeared to them to be the loss of another "daddy." I suffered, my children suffered, and I made more wrong decisions than right ones in those days. Thankfully, I had met the Lord during that season and my heart began to heal, but I wasn't yet renewed to God's Word and didn't know how willing He was to help me. I continued to do all I knew to do to help myself and the girls. I often left them with sitters as I pursued work, relationships and studying to find a road through yet another tunnel that had seemed to have absolutely no light at all at its end.

My heart was to seek a better life, but I made way too many wrong choices in pursuing that goal. Both of my daughters would tell you that I was mostly MIA (Missing In Action) in their youth. I always saw to it that they were well cared for but that's not the same as rearing them myself. We all suffered because of my bad choices, especially Michele. Later in life she told me that she felt that I had abandoned her, too. That pierced my heart. I could see that in those early years I had been so blinded by the immediate needs that I missed many of the necessities.

God said that as long as there is day and night the entire earth will operate on the sowing and reaping principle. While the earth remains, Seedtime and harvest, Cold and heat, Winter and summer, And day and night Shall not cease (Genesis 8:22). That principle works for evil as well as for good and I now see that much of the sorrow I have reaped in my family over the years was the fruit of seeds of neglect I sowed earlier in life. What you plant, will come up, and the wise person learns to plant things that bring life and peace. I spent much of my twenties living for the moment which crippled me and my daughters, and will cripple you as well. I now know that living life with eternity in view is an important part of staying on the right path and living the abundant life.

About a year after my long-term relationship ended, I met another man who lived in New York. His job brought him to Indiana occasionally and we began seeing each other regularly. After a couple of months of trying to handle the challenges of a long-distance relationship, he asked me to move to New York. I was certainly ready for a change and New York sounded really glamorous to me. I agreed, quit my job and made plans to move. Marci did not want to go to New York and began talking to her father about living with him. I was totally opposed to that idea and fought with both her and him for her to stay with me. That was a very difficult time for me. I wanted Marci with me, but ultimately, she moved in with her dad and Michele and I moved to New York.

I thought New York was wonderful. Everything seemed bigger than life there. My new relationship went well for about eight months and then began to fall apart rapidly. Michele began hanging out with the wrong crowd and began skipping school. She was rebellious and her friends introduced her to smoking pot. My new boyfriend had no children and Michele's continual disobedience was a constant source of contention between us. The strain became too much and we broke up. While I was dealing with that break-up Michele was caught shoplifting with several of her questionable friends. Since she had no prior record, the police were going to let her go with a stern and terrifying reprimand, but an officer I knew from our local precinct strongly suggested that I agree for Michele to go to juvenile detention for three months. He saw that Michele was vulnerable and wanted attention, even if it came from the wrong people, and that she was easily led astray. He said that he'd oversee the process and felt that the experience would save her from a life of crime. That seemed extreme to me, but he was very persuasive and I reluctantly agreed. Michele was sent to an all-female juvenile detention center in Albany, New York that had a special program that focused on crime prevention.

# CHAPTER THREE

# Angelic Intervention

It was a cold winter day and I needed to drive from my home in Harrison to Albany. I was going to visit Michele at the detention center. It was lightly snowing when I left, but about 70 miles from my destination I drove into blizzard type conditions. I was only allowed to visit her one day a week so I was determined to make the trip. In good weather, it was about a 2 ½ hour drive to Albany, but that day it was taking considerably longer.

The snow was blinding and many cars were pulled off the side of the road but I was still able to move slowly, so I continued. As I drove on a nearly empty interstate highway, I passed a man walking on the side of the road. He was wearing lightweight military camouflage and was holding a backpack next to his chest. He made no attempt to get my attention and I passed him. Approximately a quarter mile further, I felt a prompting from the Lord to pick him up so I pulled over to the side of the road and stopped. It was snowing so hard I couldn't see him in my rearview mirror but in about a minute he came into view. I waited for him to reach me. When he approached the car, he came around to the driver's side window. I rolled it down and before I spoke, he did. With a gentle, quiet voice he asked if he could help me. Could he help me?! What a strange question! It seemed obvious that he was the one who needed help. I said no, I was okay, but that I had stopped to give him a ride if he wanted one. He thanked me and said yes, he would appreciate a ride, walked around the front of the car, and got into the passenger side front seat.

I noticed immediately that he had no hat or gloves and that his fingers were blue. I turned up the heat in the car and started driving again slowly. The weather didn't allow me to go much more than 15-20 miles per hour. My new passenger took off his boots and socks and his toes were blue, too. He thanked me many times for picking him up and told me that several others had driven passed him but no one else stopped. I told him that my name was Linda and he responded by saying that he was so glad to meet me and again thanked me for the ride, but didn't offer me his name and I didn't ask. We initially had no conversation other than me asking where he was going so I would know how far I could take him. He told me that he was going to Boston. We were about 35 miles away from the point where I would have to leave him and go in a different direction. Because of the weather, that 35-mile ride took nearly two hours. I told him that I was going to Albany and where I would leave him off.

My new passenger had the blondest hair and bluest eyes I had ever seen and was very kind and considerate. He was not inappropriate in any way. After about ten minutes, as he began to get warm, he began to talk. He told me that he had just completed service in Hawaii and had flown into Newark to go to his next assignment. He said that there was no transportation available for him there. None of that made sense to me, especially since we were probably 100 miles from Newark, and there were usually multiple choices of transportation available at the airport, but I kindly listened to him and didn't ask questions. I remember quietly praying in tongues and having no fear and feeling totally safe and at ease. I continued driving slowly paying close attention to the road because it was nearly impossible to see through the heavy, blinding snow. Our conversation was minimal. My passenger would sometimes hum songs that were unfamiliar to me.

Approximately twenty minutes after picking the man up, I came upon a rest area and told him that I needed to stop and make a call. I thought it best to call the people who were expecting me in Albany. I wanted to give them an update on my situation. I knew I would arrive at the center very late and didn't want to lose my visitation privileges with Michele. I explained all of that to my passenger as I pulled into the rest area. It was before the age of cell phones and I needed to use a pay phone. I parked the car as close as possible to a bank of phone booths.

As I parked, I noticed that my passenger's clothes were still wet and he was just beginning to warm up. I got out of the car, grabbed some loose change from the console and my coat from the backseat and walked quickly to one of the phone booths to make the call. For some odd and unknown reason that I still question to this day, I left the car running with my purse, ID, money, and credit cards in the front seat. I was in the phone booth talking when I came to the stark realization that I left my purse and everything in it with a total stranger. If he decided to take off, I was far enough from the car that there was no way I could reach it and I would be stranded in a snow storm without even so much as a quarter to make another call for help. I remember just praying in tongues and receiving peace.

The call went well and I was surprised and thankful that the facility granted me favor. On a previous visit with Michele, I noticed that parents of another girl at the center arrived less than fifteen minutes before visiting hours were over and the management would not give them extra time. They had to leave at the end of the scheduled visitation. The manager on duty told me to take my time and drive safely. He said that he would grant an exception, and allow me my regular visit with Michele when I arrived. I finished the call and returned to the car. I put my coat in the back and, when I sat in the driver's seat, I glanced at my purse. It appeared to be untouched and exactly as I had left it. I carefully pulled back out on to the interstate and continued driving saying only that I had received the favor I wanted. My passenger responded, "I knew you would."

Once we were back on the road, I was quiet, not talking at all, which is not normal for me. I was paying careful attention to my driving. There was no other traffic ahead of me and it was sometimes difficult to know if the car was even on the road. Shortly, the man continued talking and initiated a conversation. He asked me to tell him more about Michele and why she was in detention. I gave him a brief overview. I was more than a little bit frustrated with Michele and her continued bad behavior and that was obvious in how I described the situation. We talked for several minutes about Michele and her troubling teenage years. He seemed very interested, asked several questions about her, and told me more than once to not be consumed with the wrong she had done, but to look for the good. He made a rather peculiar comment. He told me that he could help her. I found that to be strange, but oddly, not disconcerting, and I didn't ask him what he meant. We didn't have much conversation for the remainder of the trip, but what little we did have was mostly about Michele. He encouraged me to believe that she would be okay and then he appeared to take a nap.

I finally arrived at the place where the interstate divided and I needed to go in a different direction. I pulled off the road as far as possible, told my passenger that this was as far as I could take him, and told him where he needed to go to be headed in the right direction for Boston. He put his socks and boots back on, thanked me again for the ride, and then said something very strange to me. He said that he'd see me again and would be able to return the favor. I certainly didn't understand that then, but have pondered his words many times from that day to this.

It was still snowing heavily. We said goodbye and he got out of my car. As soon as he shut the door behind him, he immediately disappeared in front of me. I was horrified! The visibility was so poor I thought perhaps I had parked too far off the road and that the car was at the edge of an embankment. I thought my passenger had fallen. I got out of the car and ran around it to see if I could help him and saw that my car was nowhere near an embankment. There was not even a slight embankment, and there was plenty of flat surface right outside the passenger door for the man to have gotten out of the car safely. Then I noticed something that astounded and overwhelmed me; actually, it was what I didn't see that astounded me. There was deep snow all along the edge of the road, at least 8-10 inches of snow, enough that it covered the tops of my boots, and there was not a single footprint anywhere in sight. There were no footprints outside the door of my car, just fresh, undisturbed snow. I looked in every direction and could see nothing. The man was nowhere in sight and there was absolutely nothing to indicate that anyone had been standing outside my car. No footprints, no man, just pure, white, drifting snow.

I walked around the front of my car, circled it completely, and returned to the passenger side door. The only footprints I saw in the snow were my own and they were beginning to fill up with snow. It was freezing cold and my coat was in the backseat of my car but I stood there by the door the man exited literally unable to move. I was trembling, but not from the cold; actually, a warm and comforting heat came over my entire body. I don't know how long I stood there, but probably at least 3-4 minutes. My heart was racing. I kept looking for the man who was nowhere to be found. No man, no footprints, no sign that he was ever there at all. My strange passenger had completely disappeared; he was nowhere in sight. My only explanation is he was an angel.

After a few minutes I got back into my car and sat there about another 10 minutes, thanking God, asking Him if the man was an angel and if so, what was his purpose in visiting me. I kept pondering the man's last words to me about helping Michele, seeing me again and returning the favor. I didn't hear anything definitive from the Lord then but was totally saturated in peace. I finally continued on my way to Albany filled with an indescribable joy.

I don't have answers to those questions, but I am fully persuaded that God sent me a heavenly messenger, a blonde-haired, blue-eyed messenger, to help me believe in a realm far more real than the one in which we live. I have endeavored from that day to this to be very aware of spiritual things and to live my life seated in heavenly places with Jesus. And raised us up together, and made us sit together in the heavenly places in Christ Jesus (Ephesians 2:6).

Seeing the angel definitely strengthened my faith in the reality and power of the spiritual world and caused me to begin being more and more dependent on living my life from that place on the other side of time. On that day specifically, I believe the angel helped me get some unprecedented favor with the detention center in extending their visiting hours for me. Even though I arrived there near the end of visitation, I was allowed a full visit with my daughter. I actually spent the night there rather than attempt the long ride home in the dark. I was going to get a hotel but was offered a parent's room at the center and Michele was allowed to stay with me. I didn't even know such accommodations were available and was grateful for the extra favor and the free place to stay. I stayed one night and headed home the next day.

Michele was released after three months and slowly picked up many of her rebellious ways, but the time at the detention center did what it was intended to do. She avoided her former friends and was never in trouble with the law again.

Marci continued living in Indiana with her father until she married and, by her choice, I had very little contact with her during those years.

# CHAPTER FOUR

# A Mother's Day I'll Never Forget

**M**ichele and I got along much better and she began to do better in school. She joined the swim team. She was tall and very lean and really excelled in the sport. Life was much better for us. In 1984 I began to sense a call of God upon my life for ministry. I was attending a strong Spirit-filled church in Nanuet, New York, and talked with my pastors about the stirring in my heart. They agreed that they saw a call of God upon me and I began praying about what I needed to do to fulfill that call. My pastors assigned me hospitality responsibilities in the church. Those responsibilities included exposure to visiting ministers. Being in that atmosphere I felt a call to get some ministerial training and licensing, and with the blessing of my pastors I moved to Cleveland, Tennessee to study. Michele moved back to Indiana. She lived with her father for a short season but he had zero tolerance for her behavior and threw her out of his house. She was hurt and felt rejected all over again. I was renting a room near school with six other students and had no place for her to stay so she moved in with my sister and her husband.

After receiving my training, I moved to Orlando, Florida, and Michele stayed in Indiana. I began attending and serving in ministry at another strong, Spirit-filled church in Orlando where I met a handsome and interesting man who volunteered in the audio department. His name was Lee. We began dating and within two months of our first date the Lord spoke to both of us about getting married, and we did. We were married in 1988.

Fast forward to 1995. Marci and Michele are both in their twenties. Marci is married and living in Indiana, Michele is still single and has moved to Orlando. Initially she lived with Lee and me, and then moved out on her own. She lived close by and I saw her occasionally. We stayed in touch by phone, and I began to be concerned by some of Michele's choices. I noticed some of her old habits beginning to raise their ugly heads again. She continued having troubling times and our relationship was tenuous at best. She had caused me more than a little bit of concern and heartache over the years but she undeniably held a place in my heart that I can only describe as inexplicable and extraordinary.

On Mother's Day that year my husband, Lee, and I went to church in the morning and afterwards met Michele and her boyfriend, Ray, for Mother's Day brunch at a lovely restaurant. I had only met Ray once before and that was for a very brief amount of time. He was a tattooed biker and definitely a little rough around the edges for my taste. He was not the kind of man I had envisioned for my daughter, but was very polite and kind and even a little charming. Michele seemed happy with him and I found him surprisingly likable. The four of us had a pleasant meal together and the conversation was cheerful.

She was very pleasant on Mother's Day and I enjoyed every minute being with her and her friend. We had a sweet time together and there was absolutely nothing out of the ordinary. Nothing in the events of that day led me to believe it would be the last time I would see this beautiful child. She seemed happy and the day was joyous. After dinner we took pictures outside the restaurant

*Michele*
*&*
*Ray*

*Michele*
*&*
*Linda*

and I remember being anxious to get them developed. We dropped the film off for developing on the way home.

A month later, John and Mary, friends of mine from Port Saint Lucie, invited me to come for a weekend visit. They were pastors and I was going to enjoy time with them and their two children, Jennifer and Joshua, and attend their church on Sunday. I had known this couple when we all lived in New York. We attended the same church there and I knew them well. I had been at the birth of both their children. I considered them to be dear friends. I had moved to Orlando about six years earlier and we had kept in touch. A few years after I moved to Florida, John received a job transfer and they moved to the Port Saint Lucie area. John had a call of God upon his life to be a pastor and Mary supported that. As John continued in his secular work, he and Mary started a church in Port Saint Lucie and John became a part-time pastor in his church. I was happy for them, encouraged them in their work at the church, and began visiting them 2 to 3 times a year. I loved this family and looked forward to those visits.

I planned to leave for my visit in Port Saint Lucie on a Saturday morning and return on Tuesday. On Friday night, before leaving on Saturday, I had a dream. In the dream I had sent each of my daughters a plane ticket to visit me. As dreams sometimes are, this one had some odd and unrealistic elements. Even though they lived in different cities, I could see the girls packing simultaneously. Each one had a suitcase laid out on a bed and, as they put items in their suitcases, the items would jump out on their own. Marci and Michele both wrestled with making the items they wanted to bring on the trip stay in their suitcases. Ultimately, they were both successful and the suitcases were properly packed and shut.

The dream changed and I was standing on the tarmac of an airport watching as a large jumbo jetliner was pulling into a gate near me. Before reaching the gate, the plane stopped and attendants rolled a metal staircase up to the front door and people began deplaning onto the tarmac and walking toward where I was standing. I was anxiously looking for my daughters. Finally, I saw them come down the staircase together, Michele ahead of Marci. They seemed to be glowing, like they were each under a light. They were each carrying their suitcase in their left hand and their plane ticket in their right. Even in the dream I thought that was curious, but the closer I looked, everyone coming off the plane appeared to be walking in a light. Each had a suitcase in their left hand and a ticket in their right. As Michele approached me, she extended her right arm. I thought she wanted to give me her ticket. I reached out to take it but before I got it, a large, strong hand reached over my right shoulder and took her ticket. I turned my head to see who was standing behind me taking Michele's ticket and all I could see was a blinding, but warm and inviting white light. The dream ended.

When I awoke, I had a strong sense that it was a spiritual dream. I prayed, asking for an interpretation, but didn't receive a quick understanding. I did some regular Saturday chores then left for Port Saint Lucie as planned and prayed in tongues most of the way. I arrived safely, had a delightful evening with my friends, and a sweet night's rest. I shared a room with their daughter, Jennifer, who was eleven years old at the time, and remember thinking about my girls being that age and wondering how different our lives would have been if I had known Jesus in their early formative years. Jennifer was very independent, much like Marci, but she had good guidance from her parents and I could see good qualities in her that my daughters lacked.

Sunday was a clear, beautiful and seemingly perfect day. We went to church and had a great service. Afterwards, we went back to the house to enjoy Mary's famous lasagna. She's Italian and a great cook; her lasagna was my favorite dish and she had made it for me that day. After lunch, I was tired and wanted to take a nap. Even to this day I rarely take naps in the afternoon, so that was a bit strange. I dismissed myself and went to Jennifer's room and lay down for about 40 minutes. In that time, I had a dream. It was the exact same dream I had on Friday night. To the best of my memory, I believe every detail of the dream was the same. When I awoke, I told my friends about the dream and asked if they had any interpretation. John prayed and we talked about it for a while and finally agreed upon the obvious, that the Lord wanted to say something to me about my children, but nothing specific came to any of our minds.

Monday morning, Mary prepared breakfast and we decided to take a day trip to Fort Lauderdale. It was a beautiful day for a drive and we had such a great time together. They were such a close-knit family and I always loved being with them. At the end of our time in Fort Lauderdale, my friends took me to a Christian bookstore. The previous year, Lee and I had attended a Gospel concert with the Brooklyn Tabernacle Choir where they produced a live recording. I had been looking for that recording to be released but hadn't yet found it. All of us made our purchases and were leaving the store when I noticed a display by the front door. It was full of cassettes of that Brooklyn Tabernacle Choir recording I had been looking for. I asked my friends to wait a moment while I purchased my copy. I was so excited to have it.

## The Call No Parent Wants to Receive

We went back to John and Mary's house and laughed and enjoyed one another. John could play the keyboard. We went into his study for a while, he played, and he and Mary and Jennifer sang. Joshua and I were an attentive audience. Later, Jennifer and I went into her room and she played with my jewelry and make-up. We were having such a good time when both of her parents came into the room and asked her to step out for a moment. She did, and they shut the door behind her. John looked very ashen and said that Lee was on the phone and had asked that they stay with me as I took the call. Later, I found out that John and Mary already knew what Lee was going to tell me which explained the look on John's face. John handed me the phone. Lee's voice was shaky and he said, "What I'm about to say is the hardest thing I will ever have to tell you." My thoughts went instantly to his mother. She had been very ill and was staying with us and I thought something had happened to Mom, but that's not what came out of Lee's mouth. He said, "Michele is dead. Ray shot her to death. You need to come home." Just three short sentences about Michele and her boyfriend, Ray; so brief, so to the point. Agonizing words that ripped my heart and changed my life forever.

I stood motionless for several seconds and prayed. John and Mary were both so kind but as shocked as I was and didn't know what to say. I didn't know what to say either. I handed the phone back to John and remember Mary grabbing both of my hands. She cried. My first thought was that I would go home and raise Michele from the dead. By this time in my walk with the Lord I had been rooted and grounded in the Word of Faith and truly believed that nothing was impossible for God. I told my friends my plans and started getting my things together to go. With great wisdom and fatherly kindness, John took me to the kitchen table and began to talk to me. He and Mary both knew Michele and they were very tender and compassionate, but had no intentions of letting me leave their house without some time to process what I had just been told. I could hear Mary praying under her breath and she said over and over again, "It's okay. I promise you it's okay and you're going to be fine." I agreed with her because I thought I could raise Michele from the dead. That may seem a little random to you, but I promise you that is exactly what I intended to do and had no doubt that I could.

John and Mary were both so gentle. I am ever so grateful that neither of them jumped into a river of sorrow but stayed very calm and spoke words of comfort and life to me. They strengthened me with their compassion and I will never forget their kindness. After the call from Lee I stayed with them about two hours and then headed home. John insisted on following me, but I was confident I could make the trip alone and promised to call them as soon as I got to the house. I said my goodbyes and John prayed for me again. Mary is really petite but she gave me a hug so tight a quarterback would find it difficult to rival. I felt so loved.

I headed home and had only been on the turnpike a short distance when I felt a prompting from the Lord to pull off. I was still in Port Saint Lucie, but I followed that prompting, turned off the turnpike, and went to a convenience store located right at the exit. I didn't need anything. I had plenty of gas. I wasn't thirsty or hungry. I just felt led to pull into that parking lot. I parked and never got out of the car. I cried and prayed in tongues for several minutes. That intercession was the deepest I had ever experienced and I clearly sensed the empowering presence of God clothe me in something I can't describe. I was very aware that I was being dressed in something I can only define as holy.

When that intercession lifted, I got back on the turnpike. I was crying and put the Brooklyn Tabernacle cassette I had purchased that afternoon in the tape player. The songs comforted me and I began humming the tunes. There is one song on that cassette that I remember being my favorite at the concert. It's called, "It's Not in Vain." The lyrics say that what we do for Christ is never in vain. I have no idea how this happened, but when the recording got to that song, it played over and over again by itself. The words, "It's not in vain" echoed over and over again in my spirit.

I was about half-way home when I became very aware that Jesus was with me in the car. I didn't see Him, but His presence was tangible, powerful and comforting; it filled my car. He spoke to me, not audibly, but I heard Him in my heart. He told me not to be concerned about Michele because she was with Him. I remembered Mary's words that everything would be okay and was relieved. I knew that Michele had a genuine relationship with Jesus in her younger years. She had received Jesus while attending a Christian school and I had no doubt then that her experience was real. A few months earlier I had even witnessed a slight desire in her to turn back to Him, but I hadn't seen any evidence that she did. Prior to that moment I didn't have a heartfelt assurance that Michele had made it to heaven. Her last years had been filled with drugs, immorality and rebellion and even in the wildest stretch of my imagination I couldn't say she was living a godly lifestyle. It was unbearably torturous for me to think that she was in hell. That uncertainty was the driving force behind my desire to raise her from the dead. My encounter with Jesus was brief, probably no more than three minutes, but the after affects stayed with me for the remainder of the trip, and beyond. His words eliminated that driving urge to go home and go straight to the morgue.

I arrived home at about 11:30 p.m. and I could still sense the power and presence of Jesus with me, but I was confused and battling disbelief. Initially, Lee and I barely spoke. What could we say? He held me and we both cried. His mother was there. She cried and barely said anything either. None of us had words to wrap around the confusion and anguish we were each experiencing. We just stood together in the middle of our living room, crying and not saying a word. Mom was afraid, Lee was angry and I was numb. We offered no comfort to one another.

After several moments we sat down and I asked Lee to tell me what happened. I didn't ask him any details on the phone and I had no information except that Ray had shot Michele. Lee told me how an officer had come to the house earlier that day, about the time my friends and I were returning to Port St. Lucie from Fort Lauderdale, and told him that Michele was dead. Lee said he was told that Ray had turned himself in and confessed shooting her. The officer said that Michele's body was still in the house which was about six miles from ours. Lee insisted on going to see her to prove to himself that the woman in the house was definitely Michele. He was told that the investigating officers would not allow a family member to identify the body but someone at the scene would help him get a positive identification. They needed that for their records as well. Up to that point all they had was Ray's word that Michele was the corpse in the house.

Lee followed the officer to Ray's house where Michele and Ray had been living together. There were several police cars in the street and several sheriff deputies both inside and outside the house. Michele's car was in the driveway. Lee asked to go into the house but wasn't allowed. He told an officer that Michele had a tattoo on her right calf and asked him to go look at it and come back and describe it to him. The tattoo was a leaping dolphin. The officer did what Lee asked and came back and described the tattoo perfectly. The body inside the house was Michele's. Lee said his heart sank. He had been trying to convince himself that this was all a big mistake and Michele was somewhere safe. The officer's words put an end to that illusion. She was safe, but not in this world. I often say that she came into the world in a hurry and she left the same way. I have also often wondered if the same angel I picked up in the middle of the blizzard later helped Michele. Perhaps he is the one who escorted her to heaven.

After Lee told me about the events that led up to him calling me at my friend's house, I sat in the living room crying and staring at the walls. Mom laid down about 12:30 a.m. and Lee and I went to bed around 1:00 a.m., but I couldn't sleep.

# CHAPTER FIVE

# Extravagant Grace

I was weepy and restless. I tried to sleep but could only doze for brief moments and then was wide awake again. That happened several times over the next few hours. I finally got out of bed at 5:00 a.m., went into the kitchen, and sat at the table. We lived in a very small duplex. We didn't have a spare bedroom and Lee's mother was sleeping on the sofa bed in the living room. I couldn't turn the light on in the kitchen without disturbing her so I just sat in the dark, staring into nothingness and crying with a deep, unrelenting sorrow. I was looking for answers that weren't coming. The facts I knew were going over and over in my head. There was no reason for such a senseless act of violence and I felt rage and hatred beginning to rise up to choke the life out of me. It was swelling like a tsunami in my heart. Thoughts of revenge were beginning to flood over me and were quickly paving a dark road ahead of me.

By what I can only describe as an awakening of grace, I began to think about the depths of despair I could create for myself. Many years earlier I had made a decision to never again walk in agreement with fear or anger. Over the years, I had leaned heavily upon the Holy Spirit and disciplined myself to stay true to that commitment. My thoughts cleared and I had the presence of mind to know that I did not want to go where that road of anger would take me. Scripture says, Cease from anger, and forsake wrath: fret not thyself in any wise to do evil (Psalm 37:8). I can't say that verse came to me in that moment but I was certainly made aware that I had no part in Ray's judgment. I asked the Lord to help me let go of the anger against Ray that was trying to overtake me.

I stood up to shake off that encroaching sense of rage and remember being near the kitchen sink when everything changed. I have no words to adequately explain what happened next. God Almighty, High and Holy came into our kitchen. The force of the power of His presence seemed to take my breath away. I wanted to fall on the floor before Him in reverence, but was frozen in place; I couldn't move and I couldn't speak. It was very different than when Jesus rode in my car the night before. That was comforting. This was heart-stopping. I didn't see the Lord; He did not reveal Himself to me. It was so dark I couldn't see anything, but it was undeniable to me that Jehovah, the One that inhabits eternity, was standing directly in front of me. I couldn't move. I don't think I was breathing. His presence was all consuming power, greater than any I have ever known, and beyond description. I had often said, or thought in my heart, that I wanted to experience the power of God's presence, but I had definitely prayed way beyond my revelation. I was undeniably face-to-face with Living Love and Extravagant Grace and I thought I would die. Nothing in my humanity could comprehend or stand in His power. He had to sustain me or I would have surely dropped dead in front of Him.

What happened in the next few minutes totally and completely changed my life forever. He spoke. For decades prior to that moment I had been praying in tongues regularly, preparing my heart to be attentive to God's voice and respond to anything He asked. I knew His voice well. He did not speak audibly, but I heard Him in my heart, and every bone, every organ and tissue, and every drop of my blood heard His voice. His words reverberated throughout my entire being. He inhabited every cell in my body. Every part of me was on full alert.

God's words sounded like clashing thunder. They were firm, but filled with intense compassion. He said, "Linda, I don't want you to be angry; I want you to be grateful. Michele has been delivered from much." I would love to say that I responded to Him immediately, but that's not what happened at all. The pain was so deep and the disbelief that she was gone was so profound that I couldn't respond. Only moments before I had made the decision to push back the anger that seemed to be fiercely pulling me into a dark hole and now the Lord added that I should be grateful as well. Thankfully, I didn't say it out loud, but I briefly thought that the grateful part was an impossibly absurd request.

The Lord didn't say it again, but His words echoed over and over in my being. "Linda, I don't want you to be angry; I want you to be grateful. Michele has been delivered from much." In about a minute, in the quiet depths of my heart without saying a word, just as an act of blind obedience, I bowed my heart in submission to the Lord, the One I call Worthy, and agreed to let go of the anger. I didn't know how I was going to do that, but my heart said that I would and the grace to begin that process came as soon as I agreed to do what the Lord had asked. I breathed a deep sigh of relief and immediately my heart felt lighter. It felt like I was breathing again. I asked the Lord for His ability to be grateful because nothing in my knowledge or experience could relate to that request.

I stood silent, enjoying a gentle peace that was beginning to soothe my tormented heart. Within seconds the Lord spoke again; this time He said, "Linda, forgive Ray. I'm asking you to forgive him." I was, and still am, a minister of the Gospel and I knew that it was required of me to forgive. Again, I didn't give a ready response, but this time I answered quicker than at first. I agreed, and said out loud that I would forgive Ray, again asking the Lord for His help to do that. More peace came. My heart was beating again. I could breathe.

About three minutes later I was still standing, immobilized by the power of the presence of the One whose name is Holy, and He spoke again. Though I was standing, everything in me was bowing before Him in reverence. This time He said, "I want you to embrace Ray as a son." It felt as if my heart went stone-cold still and I could barely breathe again. After several seconds I spoke back, not in defiance, but in disbelief. "Surely," I said, "You don't require this of me? I don't even know this monster that killed Michele and I certainly don't want him in my life. Please tell me that I didn't hear You right." The presence of total power and the purest love was very real in front of me, filling the room and running all the way through me at the same time. Undeniably, it was the Lord Almighty speaking and He didn't dignify my questions with an answer. He had spoken, and yes, I heard Him correctly. I stood silent for what seemed like an eternity, but was probably closer to a minute or two. I rehearsed how my heart felt after I agreed to let go of the anger, to be grateful, and to forgive Ray. After each of those decisions I received divine assistance and peace. I had felt a freedom come from deep within my spirit and my soul was refreshed and renewed.

I was totally aware that I had the full right and authority to make the choice, and I knew that the next words out of my mouth would mark the rest of my life. I was a woman of faith and knew that I could trust the Lord. Even though I could see no imaginable way out of the senseless void I was in, I knew that I had heard from the ever eternal One and that obeying Him was my only way out of the abyss that was trying to destroy me. I didn't allow my soul to rule, and I didn't bow to my emotions; I simply made a choice. It was nothing more than an emotionless, blind-faith choice to trust God. I had walked with Him long enough to know that He would never lead me where He wouldn't keep me. I resolved by choice, not by feeling, to not be angry, to be grateful, to forgive Ray and embrace him as a son. Even though all of that seemed totally irrational and impossible, I opened my mouth and said out loud, "I will." I simply said "yes" from the depths of my heart, and the rest was up to God.

As soon as I made that final choice, a flood of what felt like a rushing river of liquid grace welled up within me and seemed to saturate every cell of my being. Not only did extraordinary grace come up from within me, I was saturated in, and engulfed by, perfect and complete love and peace. It was as if I was swept up in a river of living water. It happened instantly and I felt as if I was breathing the purest air possible and was being cradled in the arms of God and all things contained in eternal life. For a few brief moments I slipped out of my reality and into His and I believe I experienced the atmosphere of heaven. God breathed His breath into me and immediately took all the fire and stench of anger, hatred, spite and revenge out of me and filled me with peace and purpose. There was a divine exchange. I didn't understand it but I was clearly aware that I had lost a daughter and gained a son.

The Presence of the Lord then lifted and I sat at the kitchen table for about another hour, basking in what had happened. I was still caught up in that living grace and quietly prayed and worshipped in tongues. I was thankful, truly thankful, and I was genuinely saturated in a peace that passes all understanding. That entire encounter with God only lasted a few minutes but the effects are still with me to this day.

My decisions were made but I knew I needed to follow through with an action. When the sun came up and filled the kitchen with light I sat down and wrote Ray a letter. I told him that I forgave him and that I could only do that because of the love and grace of Jesus Christ. I told him to ask Jesus to help him, and He would, and that I would pray for him. I didn't tell him about embracing him as a son. Actually, he was already released from jail, twenty-four years later, before he knew that part of what the Lord asked me that morning. My actions had demonstrated my obedience to that word decades before I told him.

By the time Lee got up, my heart was healed. I tried explaining what had happened but he didn't receive the same download of grace I did and my words went completely over his head. He was still very angry and it was twelve more years before he was able to forgive Ray, and another eight after that before he even began to acknowledge that I would embrace him as a son. Thankfully, he was eventually able to do both.

Later that day I called the church we attended and sent my letter to the jail by way of a pastor in charge of prison ministry. He later told me that on his next visit to the jail he read the letter to Ray and prayed with him. He said that Ray thanked him but had no other comment. The pastor left the letter with a corrections officer because Ray wasn't allowed to have it at that time.

# CHAPTER SIX

# That Was the End of That!

Two days after my encounter with God I was still caught in a bubble of grace. The last thing I wanted to do was make preparations for Michele's funeral. We didn't yet have a date that we could hold her services because there was an active, open homicide investigation. Michele's body had not yet been released but it was nonetheless necessary to work on the arrangements. Lee spent much of the morning making calls. Everything was so surreal. I felt like I was watching a movie.

Late that morning two officers from the Orange County Sheriff's Department came to our house, along with a woman they introduced as my court appointed victim's advocate. We invited them in and we all sat down in the living room. One officer did most of the talking while the second officer took notes. They expressed their sympathy for Michele's death and told us that they had come to answer any questions we may have about what had happened, or what to expect going forward. They said that they would honestly answer any question they were asked to the best of their ability, but that they would offer no information. They said that due to the brutality of the crime they wanted us to be in charge of how much we wanted to know. I appreciated that and took it as my guide. By choice I knew very little about the details of the crime until Ray and I sat down together to write this book. Thankfully, by then, my heart had over twenty-four years to heal.

I only remember asking one question that day. I asked if Michele had suffered. I was told that the preliminary autopsy report indicated that the second shot was the fatal one but that it would be several weeks before the report would be finalized. I then knew that Michele had been shot at least twice. To this day I have not read that final report. To me, keeping a record of wrong would go against the gift of grace I had received.

I think Lee asked questions but neither he nor I remember what those questions were, or the answers. Lee's mother asked a question or two as well, and again there is no remembrance of those questions or the answers.

Then our newly appointed court appointed victim's advocate spoke and told us what her responsibilities were. She said that she would be in regular contact with us throughout the legal process ahead of us and was available for any assistance we may need. She would be with us through the court proceedings and would help us with trauma and grief counselling. She was a sweet woman with a meek spirit. I liked her immediately but didn't feel we had a need for her services. She obviously thought otherwise and worked tirelessly to get me to go for psychiatric help. She was convinced that I was in shock and needed therapy.

Although I was truly doing remarkably well, I did have one meltdown the morning of Michele's funeral. I was on the phone with another friend also named John and I said over and over to him, "I can't do this. I can't do this," meaning that I couldn't go to the funeral. I remember his words to this day. They were sharp and caustic, but exactly what I needed. He said, "What? We're going to bury your daughter and you're going to be a no show? I don't think so. Get dressed." His words pierced through the tremendous sorrow that was once again trying to grip my heart. I've had saddened moments of missing Michele but from that day to this I have never again been tormented with grief. That was the end of that! I am so grateful for strong, godly friends who speak truth in due season. Thank you, John Lewis.

We buried Michele and life continued. The long court proceedings ahead seemed monumental but my heart was whole and I was strong. My advocate called regularly, constantly offering the emotional support she thought I so desperately needed. Nothing I said could convince her that I didn't need those services.

# The Visit

About two months after Michele's death, my advocate called to tell me that, as a part of my victim's rights, I could have one visit with Ray to confront him before his trial. She asked if I wanted that visit and I said, yes. She said that she would make those arrangements.

On the day of the visit my advocate met Lee and I at the Orange County jail where Ray was incarcerated. She tried to prepare me for the visit, saying that I could say anything to Ray that I wanted and encouraged me to vent my emotions. She said if Ray became violent, there would be officers to take care of it immediately. I was allowed one hour, or whenever I wanted to leave, whichever came first. She waited with Lee in the lobby and I was escorted through security and taken by a pleasant Corrections Officer to a small room. He told me that he was sorry for my loss and that he would stay with me. The room was behind a half glass wall and had one table with two chairs. I sat down and the officer left and stood outside the room watching me through the glass. There was an acrid smell and the atmosphere was thick with terror. I remember praying in tongues incessantly.

In about five minutes another officer brought Ray to the room. He had lost weight since I had seen him on Mother's Day and the prison uniform he was wearing hung loosely on his frail frame. His face was drawn and he had deep, dark circles under his eyes. He looked so pitiful and afraid. His hands were shackled behind his back and his ankles were shackled together, too. The officer sat Ray down at the table directly across from me and I asked him to please unshackle Ray. He immediately said, "I can't do that, ma'am." I asked again and added that I was not afraid and wasn't there to hurt Ray. The officer hesitated and appeared to get approval from the first officer who was standing in the hall. He paused briefly, then unshackled Ray's hands but left his feet bound. He then left the room, joined the first officer standing in the hallway, and stayed there throughout our entire visit.

I remember very little of my conversation with Ray that day. There were long moments of silence and he didn't speak unless I spoke first. I do remember asking him why he killed Michele and without looking at me, and fighting back tears, he said over and over again that he didn't mean to do it. He told me that he loved her and said he was sorry. I needed to hear that. My decision to forgive him had been made, but if he wasn't remorseful, I knew that having any kind of relationship with him would be tortuous for me. I told to him to please run to Jesus and he said that he had a Bible and was reading it. I was pleased.

I cried uncontrollably much of the time but not because of the loss of Michele. By the time of our visit my heart was healed. I cried because I was fully aware that the Lord was extracting from me the promise I had made Him in our kitchen that I would embrace Ray as a son. How could I possibly do that? I could see absolutely no way that could happen. My flesh wanted to leave that room and never look back but my spirit was singing, "Grace, grace, wonderful grace, sent down from the Father above." I was comforted, but still very confused about what this relationship would look like.

At one point I reached across the table to take Ray's hands. I noticed the officers in the hall begin to move toward the door. Ray reached back. The officers remained in the hall. I held Ray's hands briefly and told him again much of what I had said in the letter I had written to him. I told him that God loved him and I forgave him. About 45 minutes had passed and I then nodded to the officers in the hall to indicate that I was ready to go. They both came into the room. The one who escorted Ray in had him stand up and started to shackle him again. I asked if I could please give Ray a hug and got an immediate no, but again the officer relented. Both officers stood close by and I hugged Ray. I felt him tremble. He didn't respond; he just stood still with his arms at his side. I pulled back, looked him in the eyes, and told him again that I forgave him. He dropped his head and said, "thank you" and was then taken from the room. As he was being escorted away, I yielded once again to God and chose to release to Ray the same grace that had been extended to me. I made a heart choice to no longer find fault in him. Grace was indeed greater than his sin.

The officer who originally escorted me began leading me back to the lobby. He was so kind and said, "I don't know how you can do that, ma'am." I told him that without Jesus I couldn't, but he clearly didn't understand. I didn't have time to water that seed, but I definitely planted it. Trustfully, another of the Lord's laborers has harvested it by now.

Back in the lobby Lee hugged me and my advocate only wanted to know if I had let Ray have it. She was still fully convinced that I was in shock and needed an emotional release. She was very disappointed with my response.

That was the last time I saw Ray until the day he was released and Lee and I picked him up from prison. I made numerous attempts to get visitation rights. I reapplied every time he changed facilities but the State constantly refused my requests.

# CHAPTER SEVEN

# A Plea Deal

On October 3, 1995, approximately three weeks before Ray's trial was scheduled to begin, I received a call early in the morning from my advocate. I remember the date well because it was the anniversary of my father's death. She told me that the prosecution for the State was considering a plea and they would like me to take a conference call to discuss the possible terms. I agreed, and we set a time to talk later that day. I was at home and was put on a call with Ray's attorney, an attorney for the State and a judge. There were other voices in the background. I believe my advocate was there but she didn't speak on the call, and there were court clerks perhaps, I don't know.

The attorney for the State spoke first. He began by telling me that our conversation was being recorded and asked my permission to continue. I agreed. He then said that he was sorry for my loss, and introduced me to the other people on the call. The attorney told me that at the request of Ray's attorney they were discussing a possible plea agreement to present to Ray to avoid the emotional cost to me and the financial burden of a trial. He said that it was important to all of them present on the call that I understood the process and told me I had the right to give input into what consequences Ray would pay for killing Michele. He made it clear that I could ask any question at any time and make any comments I'd like, and that anything I said would be recorded and become a part of their permanent file.

The attorney for the State continued and told me that Ray had been charged with premeditated, first-degree murder and that there were only two possible sentences for that charge. He said that the State was convinced they had more than enough evidence to see Ray convicted of those charges and said that either sentence would assure that he would never take someone else's daughter's life. The choices were the death penalty or life without parole. I was told that if I insisted on one or the other, my wishes would be favorably considered and they would take another look at the request by Ray's attorney to offer a plea.

I was asked which of the two sentences I preferred. I didn't hesitate; I said that I wanted neither. It was very quiet on the other end of the phone and shortly Ray's attorney spoke. His attorney was a woman with a soft voice. She said almost exactly what the first attorney had said, repeating it slowly, carefully articulating her words. She asked me if I understood the charges and my choices of sentence and I assured her that I did. She then asked me again which of the two mandatory sentences I preferred

and I again said, "Neither." She seemed pleasantly surprised. It appeared to me that she thought I wouldn't
agree to a plea deal and felt obligated to go over the original charges and choices once again. She reiterated that if
Ray's charges held, I only had the two choices presented
to me, the death penalty or life without parole. She asked
me if I understood. I assured her that I understood and
she then asked if I was open to going forward with a plea
deal. I said yes and asked her to please work something
else out because I wanted Ray to have the opportunity for
parole. She seemed to be in disbelief and told me that they
would call me back.

We hung up and I waited and prayed. I didn't know
exactly what I wanted for Ray other than for him to have
an opportunity to be a free man again. It was well over an
hour before I received that return call. When the call came,
the attorney for the State spoke and said that he and Ray's
attorney had come to an agreement and that the State was
willing to reduce Ray's charge and offer him a plea deal
if I agreed to the terms. He told me that the plea would
reduce Ray's charge from premeditated, first-degree murder to second-degree murder with a firearm. That charge
came with a sentence of thirty-seven years, with three
years mandatory, and the possibility of earning gain-time
and parole. I asked if there were other choices and the
State's attorney said firmly that he was not willing to go for
a lesser charge and then spoke for me and said that I didn't

want anything lesser either. He frankly told me that in his opinion the reduced sentence didn't match the crime. It was very apparent he wasn't willing to negotiate further. I pondered briefly. I was basically getting what I wanted; I wanted Ray to pay for his crime but not be incarcerated for life. I felt peace and agreed to the terms. I was told Ray would be presented with the plea and I would be notified on whether he accepted it or wanted to go to trial.

Later that day my advocate called and told me to meet her at the Orange County courthouse a few days later to stand before the judge and tell him face-to-face my decision concerning the pending plea deal. I'm still not clear why I had to do that, but I followed instructions and met her there. She was very kind and caring and told me as we walked into the courthouse that it was not too late for me to ask for Ray's original charges to stand and the original choices of sentence to remain.

Orlando now has a new, sleek, contemporary courthouse, but then County court was held in an old-style, musty courtroom with dark wood benches and dark paneling, much like you might see on an old Perry Mason rerun. We sat in a hallway waiting our turn to enter the courtroom. My advocate told me that law students would be in the gallery observing the work of the judge that day. When I was taken into his courtroom, I was asked to stand at a small podium directly in front of the judge. Before he addressed me, the judge spoke directly to the law students.

He had obviously been briefed on what had previously transpired. He told them they needed to pay careful attention because if they chose to serve in law all of their lives, they would probably never again witness what they were about to see. He said this was a first for him.

My time before the court was brief. The judge briskly and curtly read the details of Ray's crime, his charges, my relationship to the victim, what had transpired between the attorneys and the details of the proposed plea. It was all rather cold and so very matter-of-fact. He asked me if I fully understood the terms of the plea that was to be offered to Ray and asked if I agreed. He also asked if I had anything I wanted to say to the court. I told him that I did understand the terms of the plea and that I did agree. I also said that I had a request. I told him that I had forgiven Ray and that I wanted mercy for him and asked if there were other options for his sentence. He snapped back and in a rather terse tone said that justice was being served and no other options were applicable. I cried. I thanked him for the opportunity to express my desires to the court and my advocate then led me out of the room past the law students. Some of them were crying, too.

On the sidewalk outside the court, my advocate told me that she felt Ray would surely accept the plea, and if he did, this would be goodbye for us. This would be the official end to her court-appointed responsibilities with me. She had been very present in my life for several months and I had grown fond of her. She asked me to confirm that I had her phone number and extracted a promise that I would call if I needed help of any kind or wanted to take advantage of the free psychological services she had offered me. Nothing I ever said or did persuaded her that I was truly alright. My responses during the entire process were clearly a first in her professional career. On numerous occasions prior to that day she had expressed her genuine concern for me. She felt I was in the worst case of denial she had ever encountered and that I needed long-term psychiatric help. She reminded me that she could make those services available to me for free and told me that she was adding two years to the original expiration date of those services in my file and for me not to hesitate to take advantage of them. I never did. I didn't need to. We parted and as I walked to my car alone, I thanked the Lord out loud that I was better than alright. I was healed and whole.

I wasn't home two days later when the call from the State's attorney came; it went to voicemail. He left a simple message. "Mrs. Markowitz, you have been spared the agony of a trial. Mr. Ciaramaglia has accepted the plea and will be officially charged with second-degree murder with a firearm and be sentenced to thirty-seven years, with three years mandatory." I listened to the message twice. There was no rejoicing. My heart ached because I knew that the script for Ray's next several years was now written and his future was dark and would certainly be marked with hardship and sadness.

I received one more call from my advocate. She called on October 13, 1995 to tell me that Ray had been officially charged with the lesser charge of second-degree murder with a firearm and had been sentenced. She said that he would soon be moved from his current location to an interim center to await a permanent placement in the State penal system and added that I could now be at peace and put all of that behind me. Little did she know. I was not told where Ray would be moved. At that point I didn't know where he stood with the Lord and I simply trusted God to take care of him. It was time for both of us to move on into some unknown territory.

I met Ray's mother, Mary, once. She lived in Boston but came to Florida after Michele's death to see Ray and to deal with matters concerning his house and personal belongings. She called and told me how sorry she was for what Ray had done. She told me again and again that she didn't raise him that way. I told her that I had forgiven him and asked her if we could meet. She was a little hesitant, but agreed. Our time together was brief. She seemed very nervous and didn't know what to say or how to treat me. I basically made small talk and asked if we could keep in touch. She agreed and gave me her phone number. She was pleasant to me, but was clearly a broken and angry woman and had not found her peace at that time. I tried, but couldn't help her. She wasn't ready.

Later, I asked Mary for Ray's address. She gave it to me and I began writing to him. At first, that was awkward for both of us and he rarely responded. Initially, I wrote about once every other month, slowly trying to develop a relationship with him. Eventually he did write back. He's a gifted artist and would sometimes send a drawing he had made. Much later we began talking on the phone. The last several years of his sentence we had a weekly scheduled call time when he would call me collect. Those calls were important to me and I tried to make sure I was home for them. I was traveling quite a bit for my job in those early days and always tried to let him know in advance if I wasn't going to be home and would schedule a different time to talk. Those calls became a lifeline for both of us.

I developed a long-distance relationship with Mary that continued until her death in 2007. I called her every week that I wasn't traveling. She didn't have the instantaneous relief from anger or agony that I did, but over time her heart healed and she, too, forgave Ray. At the end of Mary's life, Lee and I went to Boston to be with her, to surround her with faith and to let her know that Ray was there with her; he was there in my heart. We visited her in the hospital and she was unconscious during our entire visit, but I'm confident that she heard every word spoken. She passed away two days later and I believe she left this earth with great peace.

After Mary's passing, something remarkable happened. Ray began sending me a Mother's Day card every year. I had not yet told him that the Lord asked me to embrace him as a son, but apparently, He was dealing with his heart as well.

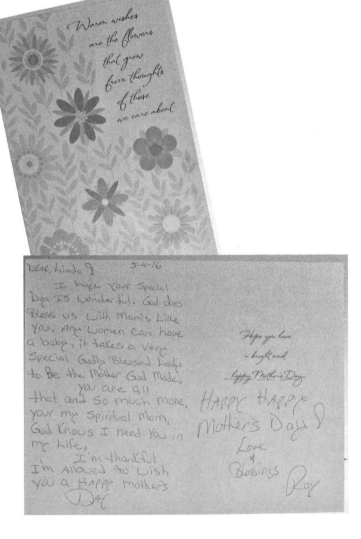

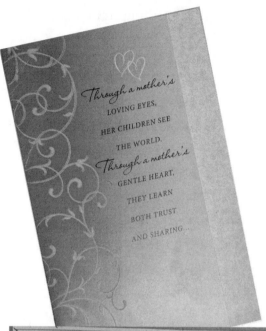

Through a mother's
LOVING EYES,
HER CHILDREN SEE
THE WORLD.
Through a mother's
GENTLE HEART,
THEY LEARN
BOTH TRUST
AND SHARING...

Dear, Linda
        This Card Says
IT All Better than I'd
Ever Be ABle.

Through all
the thoughtfulness she shows
to everybody
that she knows.
They learn just what
is meant
by love and caring!

You are a Priceless
Blessing to Just Know
You, your more so
Because God Blessed
me With Being Part of
Your life.

My Life is Better as
Well as Blessed
Because You are IN IT!

Thanks for being
such a wonderful example
of what every mother
should be.

Happy Mother's Day
with Love

Have an awesome Day!

Love
&
Blessings
Ray

P.S
You are
my Spiritual
Mom.
God Knows I
needed TLC!

I also sent
as smile
Bringers, my
Little Friend!

# Ray's Story

# CHAPTER EIGHT

# Jesus Didn't Live at Our House

I was born in Boston, Massachusetts in March 1963, the youngest of three children born to Ralph L. Ciaramaglia and Mary Varone. I have an older sister named Sandy, and an older brother named Steven. We were brought up as old-school Italian Catholics, but were not necessarily a religious family. When I was young, my Ma saw to it that we went to Ash Wednesday, Palm Sunday and Easter services but rarely went at other times and never attended church regularly. As I got older, we were only in church for weddings and funerals. I believe all parents should teach their children about Jesus, take them to church and lead godly lives before them, but that was not my experience.

My first memory of knowing anything about Jesus happened when I was seven years old. I attended Sunday School at Saint Teresa's Catholic Church in Everett, Massachusetts, where I heard stories about Jesus and His sacrifice and resurrection, and colored pictures that went along with those stories. Even at that young age I felt a tangible presence of love from this Jesus I didn't even know. I somehow understood He loved me anyway and did something remarkable for me. Those stories made me feel so happy. I went home and told my Ma everything that was so big in my heart about Jesus and showed her my pictures. Her response was, "What I believe is my business. Keep that to yourself. Go out and play." I thought I was in trouble and I began thinking that I didn't even know this guy named Jesus and He'd already gotten me in trouble with Ma. I later told my dad about the stories I'd heard at Sunday School and he basically said the same thing to me that Ma did. My heart that had been so happy was now crushed and I learned very quickly that Jesus was not at our house; He lived at Saint Teresa's.

I had no godly influence at home, but at my grandparent's house, Grandpa Freddy and Grandma Jean Varone's, I was taught kindness, integrity and morality. They loved one another and always treated each other with respect. It was very different with them; I felt nurtured, safe and at peace at their house. Outside of their home I witnessed a lot of dysfunction, brokenness and violence in my family. I knew my grandparents loved me and I always looked forward to being with them because none of that was allowed in their house.

No one could cook like Grandma Jean. Going to her house was like going to a world-class buffet with endless amounts of the choicest foods to eat. We didn't need a holiday to eat good at Grandma's house. She cooked like that almost every day. Grandpa Freddy was a World War II veteran and I, as a young boy, was captivated by stories of his war adventures, especially how he captured a German SS Captain and three other German soldiers. I saw Grandpa as a super hero, especially when he would tell me about taking the SS Captain's luger and bayonet away from him. For a young boy, that was like being in the army myself, and Grandpa Freddy was in many ways bigger than life to me.

After Grandpa Freddy left the Army, he worked for Bethlehem Steel and ultimately became the vice president of the Ship Builders' Union. In our family that was like being the president of the United States. He was a big and important man in our family, and especially in my life. I learned honor, respect and responsibility from him. He had a massive heart attack in his 50's and the doctors told my grandmother he could not survive, but he pulled through and lived another 20 years. That just confirmed to me that Grandpa was a strong and important man and I always looked up to him and wanted to be like him.

Grandpa Freddy and Grandma Jean helped set my moral compass. When he died, that strong sense of goodness and morality seriously weakened in our family. Grandma Jean was the glue that held our family together and, when she died, it seemed to evaporate completely. Our family became more and more distant; pettiness began popping up and did what it always does, it corroded our unity and we began going in very different, disconnected ways.

After my grandparents died, church disappeared into my rear-view mirror and I had no further significant connection with Jesus until I was 32 years old and had committed a murder. I was on suicide watch in solitary confinement, terrified and angry. How did I get to this place?

# CHAPTER NINE

# Where Did I Go Wrong?

Without hesitation, I can definitely say that drugs were the catalyst that caused me to take Michele's life and landed me in prison. I had messed with pot off and on since the age of ten and thought I handled it well. All potheads think they're handling it well, and I was no exception. Smoking pot started me on a ride down a dark and miserable road. Pot was definitely a stepping stone to harder drugs for me. By the time I was thirteen I was using speed and hallucinogenics, and added cocaine to my habit when I was sixteen. Later, I also free-based cocaine and used barbiturates and anything else I could get my hands on. I was lost in all those drugs and they totally altered my personality.

I quit school in the twelfth grade because drugs seemed to be the most important thing in my life and education meant nothing to me. The guidance counselor tried to talk me out of quitting. He told me that quitting so close to the finish line would be something I'd regret. He was right, but I didn't agree with him then and left school anyway. I got a series of jobs, none of them lasting very long. I was too high to do my work, or was always late, or wouldn't show up at all, so I was fired repeatedly.

In my early twenties I went to work for a packing company. The owner liked me and took me under his wing. He became a father figure to me and we got along well. I really liked him and I liked my job. One day he did something petty that made me mad and I quit. That was a big mistake. I went back three days later and apologized. He was kind and said he forgave me, but that he wouldn't hire me back. I was so disappointed and very sad. I was painfully aware that my life was set on a tangent of failure, but I didn't know where to go for help. I went home from my former job that day confused and hurt and did what I always did, I got high.

I had a motorcycle accident in April of 1988. A man in a car hit me head-on. It put me in the hospital with a broken fibula and tibia on my left leg and crushed a vertebra in my neck. I was hospitalized for over a month and released with pain killers and crutches. I was given prescriptions for a hundred Percocet and a hundred Valium at a time and in short order I was abusing them.

In 1991 I received a settlement from a lawsuit over the accident. I was completely messed up and knew I needed a change and thought the settlement money was my ticket out of hell. I knew a few people in Florida, an aunt and uncle, several cousins and two friends, and decided to use my settlement money to leave Massachusetts and move to

Florida. I bought a house in Orlando, moved and found a job right away. I got a warehouse job but wanted to drive a delivery truck. I told my boss I wanted that opportunity and he told me another driver had quit that very day. I got the driving job I wanted, and a raise. I thought my plan was working; I was getting a new start.

A lot of addicts think if they move away from the familiar, they'll straighten up. I was the same. I thought that getting away from all my druggy friends and suppliers would help me go straight, but that turned out to be the furthest thing from the truth. I was an addict, and my body never stopped craving the drugs. I was only in Orlando four days before I found someone who could get me some pot. Nothing had changed with my drug habit except that now I was in a new city and needed to find new suppliers.

## The Madness Escalates

My Ma wanted to become a snowbird and come live with me in the winter. I had bought a 3-bedroom house and she came down from Massachusetts my first winter in Orlando, stayed a short while and returned home. I thought that worked out pretty well. I was glad to have her visit, and glad when it was time for her to go home. It was a nearly perfect visit. Once Ma returned to Massachusetts things got really heated between her and my brother. They were fighting constantly and he became violent with her. She had loaned me $7,000.00 to buy the house and called and told me that she was coming to live with me permanently. That wasn't in my plans, and I tried to talk her out of it, but how do you say no to a persistent mother? What was supposed to be a part-time arrangement became a permanent situation. I wasn't happy about Ma moving in, but initially, things weren't so bad. I was enjoying my new house, working a job I liked, doing my drugs and Ma pretty much took care of things at home. Ma hated drugs so I became pretty creative at hiding most of my using from her and we got along pretty well. Then things changed drastically.

In 1992 I met a girl I really liked and started dating her. Things were rocky between her and my mother from the beginning. Ma knew that my new girlfriend had a history with drugs and had previously been in a long-term relationship with a notorious cocaine dealer who had overdosed on cocaine and died. Ma would regularly pick fights with my girlfriend and she fought back. Ma told me countless times that my girl was trouble. She called her vulgar names and said she wasn't good enough for me. She begged me countless times to have nothing to do with her. Looking back, I should have listened to her, but love is blind, and I really wanted to marry this girl, and I did. We got married in February 1993 and Armageddon began in my house; the three of us were now living under one roof.

After the wedding the fights between the three of us escalated and the atmosphere in the household was always volatile. Ma was unrelenting in trying to break up my marriage and made all of our lives miserable. Ma and my wife were constantly fighting and putting me in the middle of their arguments. There was no peace in my life in those days. As dysfunctional as all of that was, I loved and honored my wife and stood up for her and that infuriated my mother. I loved Ma, too, but she kept tension raging and the more I protected my wife, the more bitter and pathetic things became between the three of us. Life was intolerable.

Once Ma realized that I wasn't giving in to her demands to leave my wife, she took an overdose of prescription pain killers and almost died. Thankfully, she survived and things became a little calmer for me, but not for long. As soon as Ma recovered, the fighting picked up again and was worse than before. Finally, eight months after I got married, Ma said she had enough. She told me that she hated me for defending my wife and that she was moving back to Massachusetts and would never speak to me again. She wanted back every dime of the $7,000.00 she had loaned me to buy the house, plus $3,000.00 to help with her expenses to relocate. I didn't have the money, but I borrowed it from my wife's grandparents.

I had bought Ma a car and on top of the car and the $10,000.00, she wanted me to pay for the rental trailer and hitch, and pack everything up for her. At that time no price seemed too high to get some peace back into my life and I did whatever she asked. The trailer was finally packed and Ma was scheduled to leave in two days. I was visiting a friend and came home to find Ma gone, along with my TV and several other expensive things. She was a co-signer on my checking account and in a few days, I began receiving notices that I had bounced checks. She had emptied our joint account and taken everything. I was broke, in debt and miserable, but in an odd sort of way, somewhat relieved. I was beginning to have hope that my wife and I could finally live a happy, peaceful life. I had sacrificed a lot for that and was longing for some normalcy in my life. Sadly, that never came.

Before my mother moved back to Massachusetts, my wife's best friend died of leukemia and unbeknownst to me, my wife began having an affair with her friend's husband. After ten months of marriage my wife left me for that man. I cannot describe the heartache and sorrow that began to overtake me. I had fought so hard for her and she cheated on me and left. I was grief-stricken and tormented and found myself drowning in agony.

During our separation, my wife's new boyfriend made life hell for me; he took me to court five times. During those same months, the Ford Motors company was trying to repossess my truck. The emotional stress and pain of loss added to loss were overwhelming. My life was spiraling out of control and I started doing harder drugs to dull the pain. Nothing mattered to me. I didn't care about anyone or anything. I was in a pit of darkness and actually didn't want to find my way out of it, I just wanted the darkness to swallow me whole.

One day I was sitting in my house with my gun in my lap, contemplating how to commit suicide. I would have killed myself that day if my cousin, Jerry, hadn't knocked on the door at that very moment. He had been worried and came to check on me. In hindsight, I can see how God spared my life that day, and how He has done it many times since. I dodged that suicide attempt, but was actually more dead than alive; I was just barely existing. Life was still a living nightmare for me and I survived by using more and more drugs to dull the pain.

# CHAPTER TEN

# Meeting Michele

I first met Michele at a mutual friend's house shortly after moving to Orlando. Michele had a serious drug problem, too, and we had several druggy friends and dealers in common. I knew her casually and saw her off and on for years. The pain of my divorce had taken a huge toll on my life. My emotions were still really raw when we met and I wasn't interested in her, or any relationship.

I have loved motorcycles ever since my dad bought me a dirt bike when I was ten years old. I remember loving the freedom I felt riding that bike. My parents had a friend who was a serious biker and I thought he and his bike were the coolest things on earth. When I was still very young, I decided that I wanted to be a biker like him when I grew up. I didn't realize that being a biker wasn't a profession. I just saw myself being cool and riding a big, loud bike, and that came to pass. I am still a biker today.

In the fall of 1994, I ran into Michele again at the same house where we originally met. I had ridden my bike there and was planning to leave the house and go to Flea World to buy saddle bags when our friend, Joe, suggested I take Michele with me. On a whim, I asked her if she wanted to go, and she agreed. We began dating that day. She had been living with her mother and stepfather and moved in with me a couple of weeks later. They were totally opposed to Michele's decision and tried to talk her out of it, but that didn't deter her; she moved in and for a while we were very happy. We had each other and our drugs. Michele made more money than I did and that worked out well for me. It was all a huge deception, but ignorantly we thought that life was good.

In the early part of 1995 Michele got pregnant. I was both thrilled and horrified. I really wanted that baby but we were both doing a lot of meth and sometimes prescription opioids, when I could get my hands on them. I knew those drugs could really mess up our kid.

I began to see some hope for a better life if we had the baby and was happy that Michele was pregnant. I was already thinking about getting a new job so I could take care of both of them. I tried to talk Michele into giving up the drugs and having the baby, but she was so undecided. One day she was happy about trying to kick the drugs and have the baby, and the next day she was convinced she couldn't do it and wanted to have an abortion. She went back and forth with that decision. She had been raised in church and was really conflicted about having an abortion. She knew it was wrong, but was convinced she had no other option. We had numerous conversations about it. I told her time and time again that I wanted her to have the baby. I promised her I'd straighten up and that I'd help us both do what was right for our kid.

Sadly, Michele was addicted to the meth and didn't think she could give up the drugs for nine months. Ultimately, the drugs won. Drugs are a wicked taskmaster. They are merciless and put demands on your flesh you don't think you can ever control. She made an appointment to have an abortion. I didn't agree with her, but gave her the money she needed for the procedure. The day before the appointment she wavered a little and I thought she was changing her mind again.

The morning the abortion was scheduled Michele and I had a huge argument. I thought she had cancelled the appointment and she told me she was going. I took her car keys and told her if she was going to keep that appointment, she was going to have to walk. I left for work angry, but thinking I had stopped her plans. That wasn't the case. She called a friend of ours who took her to the clinic and our baby died that day.

When I got home from work Michele was gone. My heart sunk because I knew where she had gone. In about three hours she walked in the door with our friend. She was so pale; she looked like a ghost. She was shaking and in a lot of pain. I was furious and I threw the friend who had taken her to the clinic out of the house. I was mad and devastated, but also very worried about Michele. I took one look at her face and had so much compassion for her. She looked so pitiful. I immediately began taking care of her. I made her chicken soup but she was in too much pain to eat it.

The next day when I left for work, Michele was in bed. I made sure she had water and her pain killers. I called around 10:00 to check on her. She told me that she was glad I called because our friend was on the way over to take her back to the clinic; she was having complications. I told her I'd come and take her, but she insisted on going with our friend. That day she basically had to have the procedure done all over again. She came home looking worse than the day before. She was in unbearable pain and she could barely walk. I picked her up and carried her to the bedroom. Michele was not a petite little woman; she was nearly six feet tall. She told me to put her down because I'd hurt myself and I remember saying, "I'll hurt myself for you." I genuinely meant that. I loved her and was going to be there for her.

Time passed and, on the surface, it looked like we got through the trauma of losing the baby, but in reality, we were just using more drugs, especially meth, to numb the pain. The meth was consuming both of us and destroying our lives. Michele began to heal physically, but her heart was tormented with guilt and she was doing more meth than ever before. She blamed herself for the abortion. She blamed me. She was angry most of the time and we began fighting more, usually over nothing.

I often think about how life would have been different

if Michele and I had that baby. The sense of responsibility instilled in me by my grandparents was still very much alive and deep down I know I would have been a good father. I believe Michele would have been a wonderful mom, too. We were just so lost in sin and sadly, drugs took a high toll in our lives.

The abortion took a lot out of both of us. Michele was angrier and I was less tolerant of her moods. We were doing more meth than before and we began arguing more. We didn't have violent fights. We were never physically abusive with each other, but we certainly had heated discussions, often over things that made no sense. I was so messed up with the meth that in a two-day period of time I tiled the floor, walls and ceiling in my bathroom. Instead of replacing all of the tiles, the entire room could have been cleaned with a garden hose instead. I had always taken really good care of my house and that's something I would have never done if I were straight. Michele was angry again and told me I was nuts. She was right. I was out of my mind, lost in drugs. I didn't really care about the house, or anything else. Again, my life was spinning out of control.

## The Day That Changed Everything

It was June 11, 1995 and Michele and I went back to our mutual friend's house for their youngest son's birthday party. Before we left the house, Michele was agitated and in an argumentative mood. She was still troubled over the abortion and told me not to say anything to anyone about it, or about our conflict over it. We arrived at the party about 5:00 p.m. We went in and I gave the birthday boy $50.00 for his birthday. Michele asked me how much I had given him and she got upset about the amount. That added to what was already eating at her and I knew an argument was brewing. Joe said we were acting like we'd been married for 50 years and told us to cut it out. He and I got a beer and went into the living room. Michele was in the kitchen with Joe's wife, Lou.

In the living room I told Joe that I felt really lost and couldn't understand why I was so down. I told him I was sitting in my backyard the day before crying and both of my dogs came and put their heads on my lap. I didn't have wimpy, little dogs, and yet they were very sensitive to what was going on with me. I sat there with my dogs and cried for at least a half an hour. I told Joe I felt really lost and depressed. Michele heard us talking and assumed I was telling Joe about the abortion, but I never mentioned it to him. She got really mad and began yelling at me and said she was leaving. She grabbed her purse and left.

I told Joe that I couldn't figure Michele out and he told me she'd calm down and for me to hang out and have another beer. I said, "No, I gotta go." My bike was in the shop with a snapped shifting spring and I had ridden to the party with Michele in her car. She left me stranded and I was furious. Joe told me to relax and said I could take his truck and use it as long as I needed it. Before I left, I had a brief thought to leave my gun with him, but didn't.

I left Joe's and went home and Michele wasn't there. I didn't even get out of the truck. I went back to Joe's, thinking she might have gone back there, or next door to another friend's, but she wasn't in either place. The guy next door to Joe was one of our drug dealers. I went in and asked him if he had seen Michele and he said, "No." I bought a gram of meth and some weed from him and left. I drove to the house of a guy Michele dated before dating me. She wasn't there either. I was frantic looking for her. I left there and drove past her parent's house and she wasn't there. I finally drove back home. It was about 11:15 p.m. and Michele's car was in the driveway.

I pulled Joe's truck in behind Michele's car and went into the house. She was in the kitchen pouring herself some iced tea. We began a heated discussion. I was hurt and embarrassed that she had left me at the party. I told her I didn't know what she was trying to do to me. By that time, I had taken all that meth, smoked that weed and also had taken 3 Demerol and 6 Percocet tablets. I was so angry and depressed I just wanted to go to sleep and not wake up.

What happened next is still a total blur to me. I truly do not remember exactly what happened or how things escalated the way they did. The next thing I remember is driving north. I stopped at a convenience store about fifteen miles from my home and bought a pack of Marlboros and a Coke. I then headed toward Interstate 95 and began driving south.

I wanted to die and decided that I wanted to go to the beach and shoot myself at sunrise. I kept driving south until I had a flat tire near a Port Saint Lucie exit. I got out of the truck and began walking. A Highway Patrolman stopped and asked me if I needed help. I told him that I was okay; I just had a flat tire and was going to call a buddy to bring me a spare. My loaded pistol was in plain view in the front of my pants. I don't see how the officer could have missed it, but he didn't ask about it and went on his way.

I walked to the exit, crossed over Interstate 95 and walked to a convenience store where I bought another pack of cigarettes and a Coke. I left there and walked across the street and began walking down some railroad tracks. I was confused and disoriented. The heel on my right boot broke off and the nails were stabbing the bottom of my foot but I was still high and oblivious to the pain. Later, I discovered that I had created a huge sore on my heel.

I continued walking aimlessly and came to an undeveloped housing project. There were streets and sidewalks, but no houses. I roamed around in there for a while and then walked back across the railroad tracks again. I jumped a fence and came face-to-face with a huge bull. I looked around and there were several bulls. I got out of there as quick as I could and found myself in a huge orange grove that seemed to go on forever.

My memory was starting to come back a little and I was scared. Had I done something back at the house? Everything was still so fuzzy from the drugs and I really didn't know what had happened, but I did know one thing; I wanted to die. I tried to kill myself three times in that orange grove. I remember putting my gun in my mouth and pulling the trigger. The gun didn't fire. I took it out of my mouth and pointed it to the ground and pulled the trigger again, and the gun fired normally. I put it back in my mouth and fired again; the same thing happened; the gun wouldn't discharge. I pointed the gun back toward the ground and it fired and worked perfectly. I did that a total of three times. Every time the gun was in my mouth, it failed to fire. Since I couldn't kill myself that way, and I couldn't get to the beach to kill myself at sunrise, I decided I was going to commit suicide by cop and tried to find my way out of the orange grove.

I could hear a truck coming down a road and headed in that direction. I walked out onto a dirt road and almost immediately, a truck came by and I put my thumb out for a ride. A migrant worker who spoke no English picked me up and took me to a different convenience store in Port Saint Lucie.

At the store I walked around back and saw a creek. I had four magazines of ammunition, one in the gun and three in my pocket. I threw all of the magazines and bullets in the creek. I went into the store and bought a gallon of water and a pack of cigarettes and called the Port Saint Lucie Sheriff's Department three times. I told them where I was and that I wanted to speak to an officer. It was almost an hour before anyone came.

I drank all the water, smoked several cigarettes and began to rethink committing suicide by cop. I had the pistol, but no bullets. As I sat waiting, I began to think about the officer who would answer the call. If I pulled my gun on him, he would fire at me in self-defense. Because he was trained to shoot to kill, he would kill an unarmed man and would have to live with that the rest of his life. I had known people who had committed suicide, some who were close to me, and I knew well that suicide doesn't end the pain, it just passes it on to someone else. I decided that I didn't want to do that to anyone. I didn't want to hurt anyone and before the officer arrived, I discarded the idea of pulling my empty gun on him.

By that time, I was beginning to have little flashes of Michele and what had happened at the house. I began to think I had done something horrible, but was still so high that I didn't know for sure what that was. I tried convincing myself that whatever I thought happened with Michele wasn't real, it was just a drug-induced hallucination. I had experienced hallucinations before and I blew off thoughts that I had hurt her as a trick on my mind. I wouldn't have done that. I had never laid a hand on her.

There was a picnic table in front of the store. I put my pistol and my wallet on the table and covered them with my shirt. When the officer finally arrived, I approached his cruiser and pointed to the table. I told him that under my shirt he would find an unloaded Colt 45 and my wallet that had my ID and concealed carry permit. I told him that I thought I might have shot my girlfriend, but wasn't sure.

The officer got out of the car, handcuffed me, put me in the backseat and went to the picnic table and picked up my things. He then drove me to the police station. They shackled me to a steel girder and I lay on the floor and fell asleep. They contacted the Orange County police in Orlando who sent two officers to my house. They broke in and found Michele dead on the floor.

I remember being awakened by an officer who said very frankly, "You killed your girlfriend; she's dead. Two detectives from Orlando will be picking you up and taking you back there." I was in shock. My knees were so weak I couldn't even stand up. I just stayed on the floor crying uncontrollably. How could I have done anything like that to anyone, especially to Michele? I wouldn't hurt her. She meant the world to me. Surely, this didn't happen. Prior to that day, I had no record with the law. I was a working man who got really messed up with drugs. What began as a little pot when I was ten had now turned me into a murderer. Drugs had made me into a man I didn't recognize, and I hated him.

When the two detectives arrived from Orlando, they read me my rights and put me in their car. After we left, they offered to buy me dinner, but I was in no state of mind to eat. They took me to the 33rd Street jail in Orlando and I was taken to an office and interviewed by the same two detectives. They read me my rights again and began asking me what happened. I cooperated with them and told them that Michele and I had an argument and I remembered nothing else that happened at the house except that we had a fight and that I was high and took more Percocet and Demerol before leaving the house. I genuinely remembered nothing until I was wandering in the orange grove, and even then, what I thought I was remembering was fuzzy and made no sense. To this day I don't remember shooting Michele. Thankfully, I believe that grace has erased a horrible memory.

The officers told me what had been found at the house. The facts were undeniable. Michele was dead and I had killed her. I was arrested for first-degree, premeditated murder, booked and put on suicide watch. I really was in hell now.

# CHAPTER ELEVEN

# Mercy Made Me a Deal

My early days at the 33rd Street jail are somewhat vague to me. They were the beginning of a nightmare I couldn't wake up from. I was terrified, withdrawing from drugs and definitely suicidal. I was kept in solitary confinement under suicide watch and wanted nothing more than to die.

Shortly after I was incarcerated, Michele's mother, Linda, wrote me a letter and a pastor from her church brought it to the jail and read it to me. I wish I had that letter today, but my attorney took it to use in the trial and I never saw it again. In the letter, Michele's mother told me that God loved me and that she forgave me for killing Michele. She said that she was praying for me and hoped I would meet Jesus because He was the one that helped her do that. I had only met this woman twice and really didn't know what to make of what she said. Her words both shattered my heart with sorrow and in a strange way also began to heal it at the same time. I remembered meeting Jesus in Sunday School but knew that I didn't know

Him the way she did. I couldn't forgive myself. How could she forgive me?

In solitary confinement, there was another inmate in an adjacent cell. I don't even remember his name, but he would try talking to me a little. There was a half glass wall between us and a small opening near the floor. Sound would carry enough through that opening that I could hear him but I was in no state of mind to chit chat and didn't talk much. One day, just before he was to be released from solitary confinement to go the general population, he asked me if I wanted a Bible. I sneered and told him absolutely not, but in just a short while something stirred in my chest and I began to want that Bible. Just before he left solitary confinement, I asked him if I could still have it. He asked an officer if he could give it to me and the officer agreed. That inmate then slid an open Bible under the partition to me. It was opened to the book of Psalm. I picked it up and as soon as I touched it something awakened inside me. It seemed as if that Bible was more than a book and I was happy to have it.

I had only read a little of my new Bible when Jesus began talking to me. I didn't know it was Jesus at first, but I clearly heard words in my heart and I paid attention to them. I felt so ashamed and worthless. I couldn't live with what I had done and continually wanted to die. I believe I heard Jesus say that He loved me and that He died for me. I remembered that intense love I had felt at Sunday

School at Saint Teresa's when I was seven years old and deep inside I heard that I was a treasure in His Father's heart and that they forgave me. He told me to go to the beginning of my Bible and begin reading.

That day I opened to Genesis and began to read. Over the days and weeks and months ahead I kept reading that Bible every day and slowly the terror in my heart began to lift and it felt like I could breathe again. I could sleep.

I met Jesus in the book of Job. I could relate to Job and I saw that he didn't have to stay in the hell hole he was drowning in. God turned his life around and gave him more than he had lost. Job's story filled my heart with hope and I wanted to know the One who gave Job his life back.

One day while reading Job, I heard something in my heart say, "I will take out My original blueprint and make you back to the way I created you." Somehow, I knew that voice was God speaking to me and the only way I can describe what happened next is that Mercy walked into my cell and made me a deal to rewrite my life. It was just that simple, I agreed and instantly knew that my life was changed. Jesus came into my heart that very moment and set me free. In jail I was surrounded with unspeakable evil and depravity, but I was free. There are no words to describe how that felt.

It didn't take long for the enemy to come and try to take that seed. I still battled feelings of worthlessness and depression. One day I was in my cell reading my Bible and I heard Jesus speak to me again. This time I knew it was Him. He said, "What you think is what you are, and where you'll stay." At that time, I didn't know that was a Scripture.

*...for as he thinketh in his heart, so is he (Proverbs 23:7a).*

I told Jesus that I was no good and He said, "I told you that I love you and have forgiven you. My Father will never remember your sins." Beginning that day, I tried to think better thoughts about myself, not because I yet believed them, but because Jesus told me to.

*Blessed is he whose transgression is forgiven, whose sin is covered. 2 Blessed is the man unto whom the LORD imputeth not iniquity, and in whose spirit there is no guile (Psalm 32:1-2).*

## Meeting with Linda

While I was awaiting trial, I was told that Linda had the right to see me and wanted to take advantage of that opportunity. I wasn't real keen on the idea. I could have refused her visit, but agreed to see her. I felt like I owed her that. I didn't know what I could say to her. I barely knew her. I was filled with shame and sorrow for what I had done to her and really didn't want to have to face her, but I felt in my heart that I needed to see her so I agreed to her visit. I now know that was Jesus leading me to do that, but I didn't understand that then.

The day of our meeting I was shackled and taken to a small room. Linda was already seated at a small table and the officer escorting me sat me in a chair directly across from her. As soon as she saw me, she began to cry and I was holding back tears, too. I just wanted to leave but knew I needed to hear whatever she had to say and honestly didn't know what that would be. As soon as I was seated, she asked the officer to unshackle me and that shocked both of us. He immediately said, 'No,' but she kindly asked again and he reluctantly agreed. He left my feet shackled, but unshackled my hands. He left the room and stood in a hallway just outside the door watching us through a glass partition. Another officer was standing alongside him.

I remember very little about that meeting except saying again and again that I didn't mean to kill Michele. That was the truth. Even though I was charged with premeditated murder, I truly did not intend to kill her. I can honestly say that I never had a single thought about hurting Michele in any way, and I certainly never thought of killing her. I told Linda that I was genuinely sorry, and meant it. She cried more than she talked that day but I do remember her saying again that she forgave me. Those words were comforting, but still rather surreal to me. How could she do that?

It seemed like Linda was in control of the time for the meeting because neither of the two officers watching us from the hall moved until she motioned to them that she was ready to go. One came into the room and told me to stand up. He started to shackle my hands behind my back and Linda asked if she could please give me a hug. The officer quickly told her that wasn't possible, but then oddly, changed his mind and agreed. I wasn't sure what to expect and I don't think the officer did either. He stood really close to me and the second officer came and stood in the doorway. Linda gave me a tight hug and then stood back and looked me in the eye and told me again she forgave me and said that she would pray for me. My hands were then shackled and I was taken back to my cell. That was the day that I began to trust her. I had already met Jesus and I began to see that whatever she had going on with Him was real. I wanted that.

On the way back to my cell I was crying really hard and the officer tried to calm me down. He told me that I was the luckiest man in the world to have someone forgive me for what I had done and that I needed to climb deeper into my Bible. God had sent me a Christian corrections officer. He was a good man and he checked on me often while I was in that jail.

I didn't have a trial. The prosecution for the State of Florida and my attorney worked with Linda to reach a plea deal. When my attorney presented the deal to me all I wanted to know was if Linda had agreed to the terms. I was willing to do whatever she wanted. My attorney said that Linda was 100% in agreement with what I was presented and I took the deal. In the plea deal my charges were reduced from premeditated, first-degree murder to second-degree murder with a firearm. On Friday, October 13, 1995 I was sentenced to thirty-seven years, with three years mandatory for the use of a firearm. The sentence came with the possibility of earning gain time for good behavior after I completed the mandatory period. That meant if I earned an above satisfactory mark for work and security, I could earn as many as twenty days a month off the end of my sentence.

Although I knew my original charge could have stuck and that my sentence could have been much worse, I had no peace. Reality set in and I felt so helpless and lost. I was now officially the property of the Florida Department of Corrections, possibly for as long as for the next thirty-seven years, and all I could see ahead was hopelessness. I was afraid, chronically depressed and still suicidal.

# CHAPTER TWELVE

# Life in the System

O n October 20, 1995 I was transported to the Central Florida Reception Center in Orlando to be processed into the Florida Correctional System. I remember the bus ride to the Reception Center. It was sickening and frightening, not only for me, but for all the inmates being transported that day. There were about twenty of us and none of us knew what to expect when that bus stopped. There was nearly total silence during the ride. My heart was pounding and I was terrified to find what was awaiting me.

The ride took less than an hour and when the bus drove into the secured sally-port entryway at the Center, the filth and evil in the atmosphere was almost tangible. The officers receiving us were vile and vulgar and treated us all like dirt. I felt totally hopeless and lost. Suicide wasn't off the table for me. I truly wanted to die. I felt that death would be better than being in this living hell.

I was really new in my relationship with Jesus and my soul had definitely not been renewed to His Word; unfortunately, my life reflected that. I was uncomfortable sharing my faith and felt bad about that, but kept quiet. No one around me knew that I was a Christian.

I learned quickly in prison that I had to get tough or die and I became contemptuous, aggressive, sarcastic, argumentative and vicious. In the general population I discovered that respect comes out of violence and I got into a lot of fights to protect myself and make my mark. The strong survive in prison, the weak become sex slaves for the strong. Those are just the cold and brutal facts of prison life. I certainly wasn't going to become anyone's sex slave so I worked at proving myself to be a violent force. I was able to do that, but am not proud of what I had to do to make that stand. I often asked God to forgive me for my vile and violent behavior, but continued doing what I felt I had to do to survive.

In December 1995 I was sent to Hardee Correctional Institution in Bowling Green, Florida where I was incarcerated for about a year. I continued being a force to be reckoned with and gained a reputation for being fiercely violent. It became well known in the system that I was not a man to be messed with. In 1996 I was transferred from Hardee to Desoto Correctional Institution in Arcadia, Florida where I spent the next eight years. My reputation went with me.

It was at Desoto that my relationship with Jesus began to blossom and I began living for Him. When I arrived at Desoto, I continued exhibiting my tough-guy demeanor and expressed it to everyone, including the correctional officers. One day I had an encounter with an officer and he gave me an upper cut on my jaw that broke a tooth. I was livid! I had a flash of rage and was ready to retaliate when an unexpected supernatural moment of quietness rose up in my heart. I just stood silent and the officer told me that I could either go to Medical and get a DR (Disciplinary Report) or go to my cell, rinse my mouth and shut up. A Disciplinary Report would have resulted in confinement and a loss of gain time. I knew the officer was serious so I returned to my cell and kept quiet.

Shortly after that encounter, I was looking in the mirror in my cell and I clearly heard the voice of the Lord say to me, "Open your heart; open your ears and trust Me. If an officer tells you to do something, do it, and be respectful." I recognized that voice and had no doubt that it was God. I simply agreed to do what He asked. I was learning that just saying "yes" to God gave me access to His ability to do whatever He wanted me to do. From that day on I had His grace to do anything the officers wanted, even if it was unreasonable or hard. I just made a heartfelt decision that no matter what they made me do, I'd do it for Jesus. Life in prison became a whole new experience for me beginning that day. Things dramatically changed and slowly I began to live more for the Lord and continued growing in my relationship with Him.

There was a big riot at Desoto in 2000. It happened on the recreational field. Nine officers were seriously injured and one had to be airlifted for critical care. He survived the attack, but quit the job. It was God's grace that had me off the field when the riot happened. I would have normally been there and would have been guilty by association and received the same consequences as the others. My sentence would have been lengthened considerably because I would have been disciplined like everyone else and lost all of my gain time. That was the first time I saw God do something tangible for me and I was so truly grateful. He was now real to me inside and out.

In 2004 I was transferred from Desoto to Baker Correctional Institution in Sanderson, Florida. It was at Baker that I finally died to my old man and others began to see Jesus in me. The new man I was in Christ was beginning to be noticed.

I was transferred to Century Correctional in May of 2009. Century was the most evil institution I was in. There was corruption in the officers, and the inmates were just as corrupt. One day, I was called into my inside grounds sergeant's office and he told me that I didn't have any choice in the matter and that I was now his new up-front orderly. That meant I was basically a groundskeeper and became responsible for keeping everything from the front gate to the center gate clean. The sergeant couldn't pronounce my last name and asked me where I was from. I told him I was from Massachusetts and he decided to call me "Boston." I didn't particularly like that name, but it stuck and from that day on I became known as "Boston" in the system.

Even though I was surrounded with unspeakable evil, it wasn't long before 'Boston' was respected, and not because of savage violence, but because of kindness. God's kindness began to come out of me. It was nearly effortless and He protected me. That kindness was never translated as weakness and even the most repulsive and vicious inmates left me alone. I remembered Michele telling me that I loved too much and gave too much of my heart. That person had completely disappeared in all the madness that led up to the night of her death. Sorrow for the loss of the person I used to be before I disappeared into drugs continually stalked me with unrelenting torment. Now that part of me was rising up again, though this time, not the old Ray, but now new in Christ. I became a light in the darkness of that prison. The love and kindness I had was His and it made me a completely different person.

On July 31, 2012 I was transferred to Sumter Correctional Institution in Bushnell, Florida. At Sumter I could really feel that God was real. When I had my first classification call-out, my classification officer told me that my custody rating would never go below maximum. My custody had already been reduced from maximum to medium security when I was at Century and I went from a two-man cell to an open bay dorm there, but they didn't have to honor that classification at the new institution.

I really wanted to go to the work camp but my classification officer told me that I had to be classified minimum security in order to be assigned there, and even if my security level was lowered, I would never go because of my murder conviction. I thanked her for her time and respectfully told her that she might say that now, but God could change it because He had already changed my security rating before. When I first went into the system, I was told that I would never be classified below maximum security but had previously earned minimum security with privileges. The officer dismissed me and I told her I'd see her again. As I was leaving her office, I once again felt God's tangible presence. From the day I gave my life to Him, I was always aware that He was with me, but that day was very different; it was almost as if I could touch Him. I knew that things were beginning to get better for me and I was fully persuaded that God was working on my behalf.

Sumter was a pretty violent prison, too, but thankfully, I was put in a cell block that wasn't too violent. I ran the track four to five miles every day and stayed out of trouble. Every time there was a service in the Chapel, I was there. I got a job with Pride Print and worked in the print shop, working on an upright vertical press, making $.20 an hour

(Not $20.00, $.20). I made control numbers for temporary tags for cars and motorcycles and several other government issued stickers. I could earn incremental experience raises of $.05 an hour and when I left the print shop, I was making $.50 an hour.

One day while working in the print shop an officer came up and told me I was going to do two things. He told me, first I had to go punch out, and second I needed to go back to my cell and pack all my personal property because I was going to the work camp. I was overjoyed! Just as I had believed, God had been faithful and made a way for me where there was no way. I left the main unit and was reassigned to the work camp.

About three days after I arrived at the camp, I was walking on the grounds and came upon an officer supervising several inmates who were painting the exterior of a building. I struck up a conversation with the officer and he was very friendly to me. In the conversation he asked me if I knew how to paint. I told him 'yes' and he told me to pick up a brush and help or they'd never get the job done. I started working for him that day and was on his paint detail for two years. He was good to me.

I began believing God for a gate pass so I could leave the property and He told me that He had something for me to do first. He said I was to help that officer and work for him until every building on the compound was painted, inside and out. I became that officer's right-hand man and we worked on the exteriors over a year and finally got every building painted. It looked like that was the end of my job and then orders came down that every bunk and every locker was to be painted gray. Just like the Lord had said, inside and out.

After that job I worked in the staff canteen for a while. That job was 7 days a week, and I often worked 15 to 17-hour days, but I didn't care. I was being trusted with cash, which was a really big deal, and it was better than cleaning the grounds in the heat of the day. All inmates without inside jobs were kicked out of the dorms after the 8:00 a.m. count and had to stay outside, doing yard clean-up and maintenance.

After the canteen job I finally got my gate pass. That had been my goal. God had been faithful and I was so happy, and so very grateful. I was assigned to the farm and became a heavy equipment operator. My boss came to trust me completely and I would often leave the grounds unsupervised. Sometimes I would be dropped off in an area to work alone all day. I had full clearance and, in my mind, it seemed like I was only in prison a few hours a day because I was given such liberty in my job.

At one point I was delivering food between the farm and the main unit. I was offered thousands of dollars to smuggle contraband between the two units. It would have been easy to do, but I wasn't that kind of man anymore and I never accepted those offers. I obeyed all the rules and happily worked on the farm for the remainder of my incarceration.

Finally, the end of my sentence was in sight. The day before my discharge I was called to the classification office. My heart was pounding. I had known other inmates who had been denied their release within days of discharge because of trumped up charges, and the first thing that went through my mind was perhaps the same thing was happening to me. I remember praying on the way to the office.

Once I got there, my classification officer told me that she had received a very disturbing phone call from the parents of the victim of my crime. She said they were asking permission to pick me up. I asked if there was a problem with that and the officer told me "no," but she certainly didn't know why I would allow that. In all her years on the job she had never heard of such a thing. I told her that I was good with Linda and her husband Lee coming, and after some deep thought and obvious disbelief, she hesitantly agreed. I left her office actually relieved that was the reason she called me in off my job. It was official. I was leaving tomorrow. I was hours away from freedom.

I was fully discharged on March 26, 2019. Linda and Lee picked me up at the prison. I was free, not only freed from prison, but I was completely free in Christ. I can't describe those first few moments on the outside. They were beyond words. A good friend that I've known since my early thirties, and who also knew Michele, had offered to pick me up and give me a place to live. I wanted him to come to the prison, too, and have him and Linda and Lee all be there when I got out but he was really uncomfortable about Linda and Lee and declined. He said he'd see me when they dropped me off at his place.

## The Freedom of Every Moment

Once we left Sumter, I only wanted to do one thing. I had already told Linda and Lee that I wanted my first stop to be at Michele's grave, and Lee drove us straight there. The ride took nearly two hours and I was taking in the freedom of every moment. I felt alive! I made my first cell phone call in the car and called my brother, Steven. Even though he knew about my relationship with Linda and Lee, he was still a little surprised to hear that I was in their car. Even my family members don't completely understand the great grace that is my reality.

At Michele's grave I found my closure to what I had done. I knelt down at her headstone and asked her to forgive me. I had asked so many times before but this time I knew it was the last. On her headstone are the words, "God's Grace IS Sufficient." I know that to be true and believe Michele now sees me through new eyes and truly forgives me. It's over. Regardless of what others may think or say; I know it's over. Amazing Grace has indeed saved a wretch like me.

*For thou, Lord, art good, and ready to forgive; and plenteous in mercy unto all them that call upon Thee (Psalm 86:5).*

After we left Michele's grave, Linda and Lee treated me to a bar-b-que lunch, bought me a cell phone and some new clothes, gave me some cash and took me to meet my friend. I had everything I needed to start a new life. My friend is like a brother to me and he was willing to give me a hand up and a place to stay. I love him and am so grateful for him.

After Linda and Lee left, my friend said, "I never thought I'd see you again." That startled me and I asked, "Why?" and jokingly added, "Did you think they were going to pull off the side of the road and kill me?" His response caused me to shudder. He said, "If that had been me, that's exactly what I would have done." I stood silent

*Linda, Ray and Lee*

for several seconds. I received another revelation of God's limitless love and mercy and realized that what He has freely given me is truly supernatural.

As I tell my story, I remember my friend's comment and am fully aware of how difficult it is for most people to comprehend the life I now live, and how I got here. Some have negative reactions, but I never judge anyone who rejects me or my testimony. I'm the first to admit that in the natural, it is totally unbelievable. If I were an outsider looking in, I'd have a hard time believing it, too. A hard-core drug user, murderer and violent prisoner who is now a man forgiven and completely free is the kind of stuff you read about in fiction novels, but it's my life and it's true. It may seem unbelievable, but every word I've shared with you is true.

Through the generosity of this same friend, who not only gave me a place to live, but was also willing to sell me a Harley motorcycle on a payment plan, I immediately had access to dependable transportation. I got a good job working for a good company, paid off the motorcycle and I've been moving forward ever since. God went before me and provided everything I needed at the exact time I needed it.

I am fully aware that I am where I am today solely because of the unconditional love and grace freely given to me by my Lord Jesus Christ, and the forgiveness of one woman who knew and trusted Him. Linda agreed to what

God asked despite the fact that I had brutally taken the life of her daughter. She never judged me except to judge me by the blood of Jesus and she kept in constant contact with me all the years I was in prison. I looked forward to our calls. She was always interested in what I was doing and proved to me over and over again that her commitment to God and to me were genuine. ONLY God. We both know that without Him this story wouldn't be possible and we give all the glory to Him. His mercy endures forever and for that I am thankful beyond words.

Jesus has forgiven me, saved me and made me free in Him. He has saturated me in His kindness and given me a desire to share that kindness with others. He's given me a second Mom in Linda. Over a decade before she told me that God had asked her to take me as her son, I felt that she acted like a Mom to me and I began sending her a Mother's Day card every year. Today, I call her Mom and we minister together sharing this story of extraordinary grace and the generous love of a savior who reaches into hell to deliver even the vilest of sinners. There is nothing you will ever do that will put you beyond the reach of God's love. Ask Him to take your life and do something with it. He will. I know. He did it for me, and He will do it for you.

# Forgiveness Is a Gift

# CHAPTER THIRTEEN

# There Are Lilies in the Valley

## Linda

This book tells a story of drug abuse, rage, and murder and how God's infinite grace changed all of that into something beautiful. This is a story of redemption. I know; I live my life in that redemption. Mercy and grace have rewritten the outcome of Michele's death and brought life, not only to me, but to countless others. I believe this story will bring life to you, as well.

I buried Michele when she was only 26 years old, full of untapped potential that was never realized, and full of dreams unfulfilled. On this side of that valley I can clearly see that her death hurled me into both the most horrendous, and ultimately, the most glorious time of my life.

No parent ever expects to bury a child. It's abnormal and completely foreign to the senses. Nothing prepares you for that. There's no place for burying your own child in God's plan for living the abundant life Jesus died to give us. It is a gut-wrenching and surreal experience and it forces parents to do something they are not created to do.

Trustfully, you will never have to bury a child, but it is possible that you have already, or will in the future, face tragedy in other forms. I want to give you tools that will help you find your way out of any overwhelming calamity. In circumstances like mine, and many others just as horrific and incomprehensible, I can undeniably say that there is a place of peace and joy. I know; I found it. It exists in Jesus Christ. I found Him to be a refuge and strength and a very present help in the middle of unimaginable horror. *God is our refuge and strength, A very present help in trouble (Psalm 46:1)*. I can testify from experience that He is indeed our strength in the time of trouble. But the salvation of the righteous is from the LORD;

*He is their strength in the time of trouble (Psalm 37:39).*

Attempting to deal with unexplainable tragedy and heartache on your own will only result in making wrong decisions and will produce deep heartache, confusion and unending grief. Outside of Jesus there is no end to the madness, and certainly no lasting peace. In Him, there is rest. I know. My heart is at rest and I am trusting God to use my story to help you find that place of rest for yourself.

We each have a single choice to make at the onset of trouble and anguish. The choice is simple: will we choose life or death, blessing or cursing.

*I call heaven and earth as witnesses today against you, that*
*I have set before you life and death, blessing and cursing;*
*therefore choose life, that both you and your descendants may*
*live (Deuteronomy 30:19).*

The choice we make in the face of trauma determines the future we live. I know. I am living the abundant life today because of making the right choice, at the right time, and sticking to that choice, even in the face of great opposition. This book is written to give you the courage to make the right choices, and live by them. The fruit of that is endless. I know. I live in perpetual joy.

There is rarely a day that goes by that I'm not conscious of the extraordinary river of living grace which was given to me on June 14, 1995. That river abides in me to this day and has grown exponentially over the years. I flourish in gratitude for that gift. It allows me to see life through an entirely different lens and has opened my heart to the compassion of the Lord. The psalmist was right, God's mercy truly endures forever. I have learned to love that mercy and walk humbly.

*What is good; and what doth the LORD require of thee, but*
*to do justly, and to love mercy, and to walk humbly with thy*
*God? (Micah 6:8)*

Agreeing with God in our kitchen that morning was the best decision of my life. God is looking for a people who will simply agree with Him and yield to His leading. With an honest heart I softly chose to agree with Him that day and then yielded to His grace to follow through on that decision. His grace is indeed sufficient.

*And he said unto me, My grace is sufficient for thee: for my strength is made perfect in weakness. Most gladly therefore will I rather glory in my infirmities, that the power of Christ may rest upon me (2 Corinthians 12:9).*

That grace is so real to me that I put a portion of that Scripture on Michele's grave marker. It reads, "GOD'S GRACE <u>IS</u> SUFFICIENT." When she died someone gave me a peace lily. The card included read, "There are lilies in this valley. Look for them." That profoundly affected me and I had lilies put on her grave marker as well. Truly, there are lilies in every valley we face. Today, I can see lilies everywhere, and I know that God's abundant grace is available for you to see lilies in your valley as well. Ask for His grace. You may not have it simply because you never asked.

*Yet ye have not, because ye ask not…. (James 4: 2c)*

Concerning Ray today, I can say as Pilate said to the chief priests and the people.

*I find no fault in this man (Luke 23:4).*

Ray is the son of my heart and one of my greatest joys is to see him grow in his relationship with Christ. By grace and with humility and gratitude I no longer see him as the person who took something precious away from me causing me incalculable pain, but as a child of God; loved and accepted. Today we minister together on how the power of forgiveness has the potential to turn every vile and wretched thing into something beautiful.

I have a vision in my heart. On the day Ray enters glory I see Michele and his unborn child waiting to welcome him home. They will have a glorious reunion and there will not be even a hint of sorrow or pain, just immense joy in the presence of Jesus and great gratitude for Him and His extravagant grace.

*And God shall wipe away all tears from their eyes; and there shall be no more death, neither sorrow, nor crying, neither shall there be any more pain: for the former things are passed away (Revelation 21:4).*

For as long as I live, I will endeavor to be a good steward of the message of forgiveness. It is the catalyst to the eternal, and the door that opens everything. I will teach the power of forgiveness to those who will hear, and lead those who will follow into that river where grace is unlimited and life is eternal and free. Forgiveness is the bedrock of the successful Christian life. My loudest message is, "Just agree with God. He's always right and He alone is the giver of life."

## Ray

Jesus has forgiven me, saved me and made me free in Him. He has saturated me in His kindness and given me a desire to share that kindness with others.

I have learned that God can take any sin, forgive that sin, and set you completely free from all burden and bondage of that sin. I don't carry around guilt or shame for what I've done. That doesn't mean that I'm not remorseful; I am truly remorseful. I loved Michele and deeply regret that I took her life, but Jesus has set me free from all of the stench of that sin. Once I accepted what Jesus had done for me, I was truly free. Even in prison I was fully aware that I am not a condemned man. Through what He has done for me I have received more than I deserve and have humbly given my life to Him. I am a truly grateful man. I'm not consumed with condemnation. I am truly free in Jesus.

I can honestly say that I have not wasted any of this experience. I share my story with a lot of people, and hope to be able to influence multitudes to turn to Christ by the change they see in my life. In many ways I know that I am a sign and wonder that can point men to Him. I am ever mindful that His presence is in me, and on me, wherever

I go. I want everyone to see God's grace and mercy alive in me and have that mercy draw them into a relationship with Him for themselves.

*He hath not dealt with us after our sins; nor rewarded us according to our iniquities. [11] For as the heaven is high above the earth, so great is his mercy toward them that fear him. [12]As far as the east is from the west, so far hath he removed our transgressions from us (Psalm 103:10-12).*

My testimony is that God gives grace to the undeserving and will fully deliver and restore anyone, at any time, for anything. I am living proof that mercy can rewrite your life. God took out the original blueprint He had for me and is bringing me into the place He intended all along. I am His son, and with His help, I will spend the rest of my life telling others about His Extraordinary Love and Amazing Grace. Now Jesus lives in my house.

# CHAPTER FOURTEEN

# Yielding to Grace

## Linda

Over the years many people, including some who are close to me and have been Christians for decades, have told me that they could never do what I did in forgiving Ray. Many say that even to this day. I have heard that same comment, or something similar to it, countless times. It has caused me to examine why I was able to agree with God and forgive Ray, take him as my son, and do it relatively quickly. Michele had been dead less than 48 hours when God walked into our kitchen. I've had many years to develop my response to the "Why and How" and in its simplest form, I have narrowed my answer down to two verses in the Bible.

*I delight to do thy will, O my God: yea, thy law is within my heart (Psalm 40:8).*

*Thy Word have I hid in mine heart, that I might not sin against thee (Psalm 119:11).*

I didn't make the decision to forgive Ray the moment the Lord asked me to in our kitchen that morning. Actually, that happened many years earlier when I made a heartfelt decision to build myself up on the Word of God and to allow His Word to set the compass of my life. I was baptized in the Holy Spirit the night I was saved and over time had developed a relationship with both God's Word and His Spirit. Without a life commitment to both, I'm quite sure I would have made a very different decision that morning. My relationship with God was the number one priority in my life and, even though I didn't see it then, looking back I now know that I was well prepared for that moment. For nearly two decades prior to that day I had been preparing my heart to obey God, regardless of what He asked, and regardless of the cost. At my core, I had made a commitment to meditate on the Word of God and allow it to direct my thinking and my actions. I became a literalist with the Bible and made a choice to believe the Scriptures exactly as they are written.

About three years into my salvation experience I came to a point where I realized that I had pieces of God's Word filed away in my brain, but they weren't producing much for me in my everyday life. I had my confession list and could quote Scripture claiming God's promises, but when pressure came, I continually defaulted to a totally carnal set of values. The Lord began to reveal to me that I was reacting based upon a natural belief system that was ingrained in me as a child. I did what everyone does. I reacted according to my core heart values, but those values were not rooted in Christ; they were rooted in a twisted, secular mindset. By submitting myself to training and correction I began to transform my mind and change my core beliefs. I did that by reading and memorizing the Word of God and meditating on it long enough to see things change. Whether we like it or not, our core heart values define the course of our lives. The way we think in our heart is exactly what will become reality in our lives.

*For as he thinketh in his heart, so is he (Proverbs 23:7).*

I am fully persuaded that having godly core values, submitting to a consistent infilling of the Word of God, and praying in tongues were responsible for my ability to subdue my flesh and make the right choice at the right time and yield to grace. If all of those components were not in place, I would have made very wrong choices concerning Ray and today would be a bitter, grieving mother instead of a woman filled with joy. Spending time meditating in the Word of God and learning how to co-labor with the Holy Spirit rearranged my mindset. Looking back, it was almost effortless on my part because the Word clearly knew what to do. I just needed to input it. By the day Michele died I had a firm foundation in God's Word and with His Spirit. I heard a minister once say something similar to this and find it to be true for me;

If you have the Word only, you will dry up.

If you have the Spirit only, you will blow up.

If you have them both, you will grow up.

Thankfully, my heart was right and I had both Word and Spirit working together in perfect harmony the day the Lord asked me to do something I deemed to be impossible. I am truly grateful that I had been so well trained and well prepared for that moment.

When the Word of God is engaged by the Holy Spirit, together they empower you in times of trouble. I had fed myself on Scripture for years prior to Michele's death and it was a hidden arsenal of power right there for my ready access when I needed it. The same will work for you, but you can't act on the Word of God you haven't hidden in your heart.

Another big key to my victory is this; years earlier l had learned to forgive when no one was asking and attempted to practice forgiveness in my everyday life. Giving forgiveness, even when the offender never asks, is the mark of maturity in a Christian. Unforgiveness puts us in prisons of our own making. Learning to quickly forgive when petty offenses came had strengthened me to make the right decision when I was faced with the ultimate test.

If you are one who would say that you could never do what I did in forgiving Ray, I encourage you to recheck your commitment to the value of God's Word in your life. A lack of honor for His Word will make you doubleminded and cause you to fail many tests in life.

Today I live in a peace that passes all understanding. I would never have that without my quick obedience to that seemingly impossible request from the Lord.

In hindsight, I can see that honoring Gods Word, and making it the top priority in my life, not only set me free that day, it ultimately pulled Ray up to a higher place as well. Our testimony could be a wake-up call for you. Is your relationship with God genuine, or is it a facade? Do you honor Him enough that you'll do whatever He asks, regardless of what you think or feel? I encourage you to ask and answer those questions.

## How Could You Betray Her?

When hearing my story some people say that forgiving Michele's killer is a betrayal of her and a dishonor of her memory. It's probably the number one criticism I hear. People, even some who say they are Christians, have been unkind and sometimes malicious and cruel. I've been told that I'm a disgrace to the sanctity of life and have been called hateful names. I fully understand that no one else received the divine infusion of grace and joy that I did after Michele's death, so I'm never offended by comments like that and attempt to be kind to those who apparently have no understanding of God's immense love and extravagant grace. He alone can show them truth.

I am fully persuaded in my heart that I'm honoring Michele in a way that transcends human ability. I know she is with Jesus now and that she sees as He sees. Michele can see Ray through the blood of Jesus, the same blood that rescued her, and she's grateful for Ray's redemption. There is no animosity in Michele towards Ray, no thoughts of revenge. Jesus paid the full price for her own sin, and for Ray's sin, and I know she is in full agreement with my decision and actions. Michele now knows that God forgives unconditionally, and so should we.

People who don't understand my forgiveness of Ray have missed the central point of the Gospel. Forgiveness of our sins, and the opportunity to be redeemed and restored to a relationship with God is the life source of the Gospel of Jesus Christ. The one word that describes Jesus' life, death, burial and resurrection is forgiveness. Through Jesus Christ, sin is no longer an issue with God. Jesus paid one price for all sin forever. *For by one offering he hath perfected for ever them that are sanctified (Hebrews 10:14).*

The New Testament presents the forgiveness of sins as something that is already accomplished and that the effect of our redemption is that we are no longer to be conscious of sin. Once we accept the sacrifice Jesus made for us, and make Him the Lord of our lives, we are redeemed! Redemption means that sin is eradicated, forever removed.

Did Ray fall beyond the reach of God's grace? Did his sin cause him to use up all of his chances for salvation? Thankfully, the answer is no. If he did, we all face the possibility of using up all our chances, too. Through faith in Jesus Christ, Ray was recreated. He became a totally new man. That is a gift offered to all mankind, but only those who receive the gift can enjoy its benefits. Ray ran into grace and grace received him and eradicated his sin.

In the sight of God my sin and yours is no different than Ray's. All sin separates us from God and we need a way to be one with Him. Jesus is that way. When the Father looks at those redeemed by the blood of His Son, He sees no sin. We don't have to ask Jesus to forgive our sins to be saved; He's already done that. Paul didn't tell the Philippian jailor to ask Jesus to forgive him. Paul told him to believe on what Jesus had already done and he would be saved. *And they said, Believe on the Lord Jesus Christ, and thou shalt be saved, and thy house (Acts 16:31).*

We receive the gift of salvation by confessing the Lord Jesus as Lord of our life, not our sins.

*That if thou shalt confess with thy mouth the Lord Jesus, and shalt believe in thine heart that God hath raised him from the dead, thou shalt be saved (Romans 10:9).*

It's not a person's many sins that sends them to hell; sin has already been paid for and forgiven by Jesus. It's the singular sin of not believing on Jesus and receiving His redemptive sacrifice as their own that sends a person to eternal torment.

*And when he is come, he will reprove the world of sin, and of righteousness, and of judgment: ⁹Of sin, because they believe not on me (John 16:8-9).*

"Every Christian says that forgiveness is a lovely idea, until they have something to forgive...and then, to mention the subject at all is to be greeted with howls of anger." ~*C.S. Lewis*~

I'm sure you've had more than one opportunity in life to know that there is great truth in this statement. The question of forgiveness is one we must all answer. All of us need the forgiveness of God. Some need to seek the forgiveness of others. Others of us need to grant forgiveness and release the hurt and animosity we've held onto way too long. In many cases, the people who hurt us may not know. Others may know and never face up to what they've done, or may never attempt to make things right on their part, but none of that is an excuse for us to refuse to forgive and release them.

This is a thought for you to consider. You may need to forgive God. Sometimes things don't turn out the way you want and you may be harboring unforgiveness against God because He didn't bring you something you wanted. God is always just. I've discovered in my own life that I don't always know what's best for me. When God doesn't give me what I ask for, or He gives it to me differently than I prayed, I've learned to trust in Him, resting in the assurance that He loves me and always has my best at heart.

There may be things you don't understand, but God loves you, and you can make a serious mistake that comes with serious consequences when you turn your heart away from the only One who can truly help you. If you need to, forgive God, and remember to forgive yourself, as well.

Forgiveness rarely comes as a natural first response when we've suffered a deep loss or hurt or been wounded, betrayed, rejected or humiliated, but forgiveness is required of every Christian simply because we are forgiven. "Forgive us our trespasses as we forgive others." When we do it right, forgiven people, forgive people.

Forgiveness is the healing balm for relationships and we often don't give it an opportunity to do what it's designed to do. Relationships on every level, marriage, family and business are damaged or destroyed because of a lack of forgiveness. One refuses to repent and reconcile or one refuses to forgive and reconcile. Friendships are destroyed and irretrievably broken, not because the actions are always that heinous but because our souls are petty and we are too stubborn or proud to forgive.

In today's world we are taught to hold on to hurt, to nurse it, to never forget. We are told that there is sweetness in revenge, but none of that is true. We only know peace when we truly forgive as we have been forgiven. Forgiving those who hurt us is one of God's requirements for all of His children. It also makes good sense. Instead of living in torment or walking around like a pressure cooker with a faulty lid and the potential to blow any minute, with God's grace, we can release hurtful feelings and be at peace. Jesus makes that possible. It is our glory to pass over transgressions committed against us.

*The discretion of a man deferreth his anger; and it is his glory to pass over a transgression (Proverbs 19:11* AKJV*).*

# CHAPTER FIFTEEN

# Forgiveness Is a Choice

"He that cannot forgive others breaks the bridge over which he must pass himself; for every man has need to be forgiven." ~ Thomas Fuller~

Nobody makes it through life free of hurt or personal injury. Someone, somewhere, at some point in time has hurt you, or they will. No one makes it through life free of hurt. All men suffer the pain of loss or being lied to, or lied about, betrayed, misunderstood, rejected or humiliated. For some, those hurts occur many times in their lifetime. If you don't find this to be true for yourself, you may be one of those people who needs to look back and see if perhaps you are the one dishing out the pain.

So, the question is not, will you get hurt; the question is, how are you going to respond in those situations?

We live in a society that knows and cares little about forgiveness. We are surrounded with anger, bitterness, hatred and revenge. It is nearly impossible to hear a news report that doesn't include stories about unbridled rage.

Forgiveness is a ministry not just to the people you forgive, but as an example to a world that easily harbors resentment and revenge that there is a better way.

Forgiveness is not just what the world needs; forgiveness is what changes the world.

At its core, forgiveness is a choice. It is a response of the heart that chooses to set someone free from an obligation that is the result of a wrong done against you. It is an intentional decision to obey God and is not based upon an emotion. It is based upon faith. Forgiveness is not a feeling. You will never forgive if you wait until you feel like it. The longer you harbor thoughts of unforgiveness, the more difficult it will be to get free of them.

Forgiveness in its essence is a conscious choice to release others from their sins against you so that you can be set free. It doesn't deny the pain or change the past, but it does break the cycle of bitterness that binds you to the never-ending torment of a painful yesterday. Forgiveness allows you to let go and move on. Forgiven people forgive people.

Forgiveness begins with making a quality decision to forgive. Just choose to obey God. *But if ye do not forgive, neither will your Father which is in heaven forgive your trespasses (Mark 11:26).* God cannot dry your tears or heal your wounded heart until you let go of offenses.

*Smart people know how to hold their tongue; their grandeur is to forgive and forget (Proverbs 19:11 MSG).*

True forgiveness is a tangible expression of extending to another the mercy given us by Christ. There is no quality in man that can make us more like God than to forgive, and yet on every level forgiving someone who has harmed you is one of the most difficult things to do. Forgiveness is the one single act of outward proof that we have truly been transformed by the Gospel of Jesus Christ.

Until you make the choice to forgive someone who has hurt you, and give yourself wholeheartedly to that choice, God seems distant. Once a sincere choice has been made, grace appears. I know this truth well. I could have never followed through on my decision to forgive Ray without God's boundless grace, and His grace didn't come until I made a true heartfelt commitment to forgive. I still remember clearly those gut-wrenching moments between God asking me to forgive Ray and me finally agreeing and saying, "yes." I had never known anguish like that before, or since; it seemed to be choking the life out of me. Vengeance was rising in me like a tsunami. I felt as if I were being mercilessly sucked into hell.

Thankfully, for many years prior to that day I had been preparing my heart to always agree with God. Admittedly, I didn't agree with Him instantly. If I had, I would have been spared those tortuous moments, but I did agree, and because I did, I could walk with Him. *Can two walk together, except they be agreed? (Amos 3:3)*. Grace instantly overwhelmed me. God took over and swept me up in the white waters of a river of grace. God provided what He required. He required forgiveness and gave me His grace and ability to do that. We never obey God without His full participation and assistance in the follow through. He is a good and loving Father. I learned a powerful truth in that moment, forgiveness gives and receives life.

I have come to know that true forgiveness cannot be accessed by feelings or by sheer will-power. It is apprehended by faith. I simply trusted God. True forgiveness requires believing something beyond your senses. It only becomes a practical, living reality by faith alone; faith in Jesus Christ.

I have also learned something else very powerful. I have learned how very much God loves all mankind. I am receiving ongoing revelation of how much God loves me, and I have been awakened to how much He loves others. God longs to reveal His love to all His creation and the way He does that is through His children. God's love is expressed through mankind loving one another. I didn't realize it at the time, but my obedience to forgive Ray was a demonstration of God's intense love for him. God loves everyone, regardless of what they have done, and He wants all men to come to Him. No one has ever gone so far that His love cannot reach and rescue them.

*The Lord is not slack concerning his promise, as some men count slackness; but is longsuffering to us-ward, not willing that any should perish, but that all should come to repentance (2 Peter 3:9).*

We are created in the image of our Father God. We are His seed and we have His ability to love and to forgive. We must choose to access those attributes. With the choice comes the grace.

Jesus' disciples had seen Him do many miracles and never once asked Him for faith, until He asked them to forgive a brother that trespassed against them.

*Take heed to yourselves: If thy brother trespass against thee, rebuke him; and if he repent, forgive him. ⁴ And if he trespass against thee seven times in a day, and seven times in a day turn again to thee, saying, I repent; thou shalt forgive him. ⁵ And the apostles said unto the Lord, Increase our faith (Luke 17:3-5).*

Forgiveness is the center of the Gospel; forgiveness of our sins and the opportunity to be redeemed and restored to a relationship with God. Where there is no forgiveness there is always bitterness and regret. Learning to forgive, and forgive quickly, is the key to a peaceful life. Instead of allowing bitterness or antagonism to set in we must be quick to forgive. Choose to make it a lifestyle to forgive quickly and freely simply because you have been forgiven the same way. *Freely ye have received, freely give (Matthew10:8).*

*For he shall have judgment without mercy, that hath shewed no mercy; and mercy rejoiceth against judgment (James 2:13).*

I FIND NO FAULT

God's entire kingdom runs on the seedtime and harvest principle. We will reap what we sow. The act of forgiving is our seed of obedience to God's Word. It is undeniable that when we sow mercy, we will reap mercy for ourselves. If we sow judgment, we'll reap judgment. Once we've sown our seed of forgiveness, our loving Father is faithful to grow that seed into something beautiful, turning what was intended for evil into something good.

## Is True Forgiveness Realistic?

If you have ever been on the receiving end of a painful life experience, you also know how things worked out. Many times, we try to pretend it didn't happen. Other times we fester for months or years in a kind of slow-burn mode. Still other times we may have exploded at the offending party, or retaliated in like fashion, leading to more pain and confusion all around. These are all the ways of the world, and when we react as they do, there is never a healthy resolution of the pain.

When we forgive others, we free ourselves from our own anger. Letting God into the process of forgiveness can ultimately bring us to a point where forgiveness is intuitive, making us more and more like Him.

*I, even I, am he that blotteth out thy transgressions for mine own sake, and will not remember thy sins (Isaiah 43:25).*

The idea that forgiveness means that sins are completely removed is one of the reasons why we sometimes shy away from giving forgiveness to others. Somehow, we see that in reference to our personal life forgiveness seems right, but when it comes to the same rules applying to one who has wronged us, our perspective changes.

I think the greatest and most profound statement on forgiveness ever spoken comes from Jesus as He hung on the cross. As He looked across the mocking crowd cheering His suffering, Jesus the Son of God, the One who knew no sin, the only truly innocent man who ever walked this earth, in His tortuous suffering uttered words that still echo throughout the world; *Then said Jesus, Father, forgive them; for they know not what they do (Luke 23:34).* These words spoken in unspeakable agony sweep away all our pitiful excuses. No matter what has been done to us, we have no excuse to continue in our bitterness toward anyone, or harbor a desire for revenge.

If we are going to follow Jesus, we must be able to say, "I forgive you." We must say it even to the people who hurt us deliberately and repeatedly. We must say it to those who casually and thoughtlessly wound us. We must say it to those who intentionally attack us. We must say it to those closest to us and to all who violate us, and say it as often as necessary.

Holding unforgiveness in our hearts can sometimes cause irreparable harm, and always damages us. When we refuse to forgive, God doesn't forgive us of our sins. That is a high price to pay for an attitude of justified revenge.

*For if ye forgive men their trespasses, your heavenly Father will also forgive you: <sup>15</sup> But if ye forgive not men their trespasses, neither will your Father forgive your trespasses (Matthew 6:14-15).*

# CHAPTER SIXTEEN

# Does Forgiveness Contradict Justice?

C an we have justice and forgiveness at the same time? Is it possible that accountability for violating the laws of God can work together with a practical manifestation of His mercy? Every believer in Jesus Christ who wants to live the abundant life He has promised must understand and come to terms with the issue of Biblical forgiveness. The Lord is all-knowing and full of mercy so there must be a way for justice and forgiveness to exist together. God's Word never contradicts itself and when properly understood, true forgiveness never contradicts God's justice.

On the surface it can appear that when God asks us to forgive those who have wounded or betrayed us, or stolen from us, or in some other way violated us that He's turning a blinded eye to His own code of justice. It's important that we understand His view of forgiveness. God never confuses moral responsibility with grace and forgiveness. The word 'compromise' is not in God's vocabulary and He never compromises His justice.

The idea of forgiveness sometimes conjures the thought that there are no consequences for the offender. That is often the primary reason why many avoid forgiveness, but that premise is false. Forgiveness is part of God's plan. Actually, it is the central message of the Gospel. When forgiveness is truly understood, it becomes clear that it never contradicts God's justice but it mirrors His love.

### Forgiveness deals with 3 things:

1. Damage (what was said or done)
2. Debt (resulting from the damage)
3. Cancellation of the debt

Forgiveness does not mean that the consequences of sin are cancelled. All sin will definitely be dealt with; the question is, by whom? By the offender, or by a Redeemer? The answer to that question is the heartbeat of Biblical forgiveness.

There are many misconceptions about forgiveness. In some ways, it is easier to say what forgiveness is not than what it is, so let's begin there and define what forgiveness is not.

- Forgiveness is not justifying evil.
- It is not turning a blinded eye to wickedness.
- It is not giving approval to a wrong committed.
- It is not giving permission for the abuse to continue.
- It is not making excuses for the offender's sin.

- It is not denial; it is not pretending that the situation didn't occur, or that things are other than the way they are.
- It is not refusing to press charges when a crime has been committed.
- It is not pretending that you were never wounded by the offense.
- It does not mean that you must restore the relationship to what it was before. Forgiveness and reconciliation are not the same thing.

That's a fairly concise list of what Biblical forgiveness is not. So, what is Biblical forgiveness? In the simplest terms, God's kind of forgiveness is not a violation of justice or morality; it is a release of guilt. He told us to forgive one another, as we have been forgiven. We forgive by faith, and by faith give the same grace that God has given us to those who trespass against us. Authentic forgiveness stems from a deep faith in Jesus Christ, trusting that He will never ask us to do something that He does not enable us to accomplish.

I believe there is a necessary balance in the relationship between grace and forgiveness. If we miss this balance, we will struggle throughout our spiritual walk. If we lose sight of the purpose of God's grace, we tend to hold on to offenses that can cause us to needlessly carry the weight of despair and have no peace.

The purpose of God's grace extended to us is to abolish an incalculable debt we owe and could never repay. Forgiveness cancels a debt owed.

If we have freely received God's gift of living grace, we must freely give to others. When we fail to forgive and give grace to others, we become critical, judgmental, legalistic, and ultimately hardhearted, antagonistic and bitter. You can physically see the price that unforgiveness extracts from someone refusing to forgive. I find that most people who are constantly negative, short-tempered and mean-spirited are harboring unforgiveness. They live miserable lives and are miserable to be around. Unforgiving people sabotage their own peace and sanity.

Renown psychiatrist, Dr. Carl Menenger, once said that if he could convince people in the psychiatric wards to receive forgiveness, and to give forgiveness, 75% would walk out cured in one day! Unforgiveness causes the mind to think things that aren't true and brings unrelenting torment.

The message of forgiveness is not an easy message because the subject itself means that something horrid has preceded it. Forgiveness is one of the hardest things to do because the sins that need forgiving are so hurtful and damaging. Even the very word forgiveness tells us how difficult forgiveness is. The word literally means "to let go" or "to set free."

It may appear that forgiving people who hurt you is unjust. It may seem unfair for them to receive forgiveness when you are suffocating in unbearable pain. You may ponder why they should receive freedom without having to pay for the torment they've caused, yet it is only in the forgiveness that the release of pain comes. It helps to stop and remember Calvary and the price Jesus paid to forgive you. In comparison, the forgiveness required of you is nearly microscopic.

I didn't see it for many years, but now know that forgiving Ray was a gift I gave myself. I believe that forgiving Ray helped him, but it helped me more. I've heard it said that refusing to forgive is like taking poison and expecting the other person to die. Sadly, I've seen that to be true in countless situations.

Unforgiveness is a wretched poison that brings intolerable pain and needless suffering. Unforgiveness can literally take your life. Many suffer unbearable, unending illnesses because of unforgiveness and bitterness. Unforgiveness can cripple us with infirmity. If you are suffering with a disease, I encourage you to ask the Holy Spirit if you are suppressing unforgiveness and if so, to reveal to you what to do next.

We actually do ourselves a favor when we forgive. To forgive is to set a prisoner free, and then to discover that the prisoner is you! It is unimaginable to me now what my life would be like today if I had held on to Ray's violation of my life and refused to forgive him. I would have been robbed of freedom in Christ and the abundant life Jesus died to give me.

*The thief cometh not, but for to steal, and to kill, and to destroy: I am come that they might have life, and that they might have it more abundantly (John 10:10).*

Forgiveness is a form of surrender and it expands our capacity to love. It did not happen instantaneously, but I can now say that I truly love Ray. Forgiveness, and the amazing grace that followed, transformed me from helpless to empowered by the Holy Spirit and I can now love Ray as a son, as God loves me as a daughter.

With Michele's death, and my decision concerning Ray and his responsibility for her death in my rearview mirror, I have another gift. I have the gift of wisdom that comes in hindsight. If we're smart, we learn the value in never wasting an affliction. I now know by experience that peace and joy come when we embrace opportunities to forgive. True forgiveness stops blaming, refuses to walk in agreement with anger and cancels the debt.

Forgiveness is not a violation of justice. God never will compromise His justice. Anyone who yields his heart and life to the saving grace of Jesus will not escape God's justice, but will instead have that justice paid for by another. Jesus' sacrifice was payment in full for any, and all justice due for sin. Only those who believe that by faith, and accept it to be true, will escape eternal torment and spend eternity in the presence of the One who lovingly paid that price.

*True forgiveness is a perfect blend of justice and mercy.*

# CHAPTER SEVENTEEN

# The Liberating Power of Forgiveness

God desires to bless our lives with His abundant grace and mercy and wants each of His children to live a blessed life. Unforgiveness is a bondage that chokes out the abundant life Christ promised to those who would believe. The forgiveness we have received from the Lord is infinitely greater than any forgiveness we could ever be asked to extend toward others.

It's not an exaggeration to say that if you don't know how to forgive, you don't know how to live. Forgiveness is essential if you want to live your life and not simply exist. In order to enjoy the abundant life Jesus promised, we need to be free spirit, soul and body. A large part of a blessed life is to be forgiven and to become a forgiver. There is a liberating power in forgiveness.

## Why Should I Forgive?

*I should forgive primarily because Christ commands it.* Forgiveness doesn't come naturally to our humanity. We have all been forgiven, and trustfully have forgiven others, but there is inbred in our carnal nature a tendency to self-preservation and a temptation to hold others accountable for offenses done to us. It comes easy to us to hold a grudge, allow bitterness to set in and to conjure thoughts of revenge. It's not so easy to forgive and release someone who has violated or wounded us.

*Forbearing one another, and forgiving one another, if any man have a quarrel against any: even as Christ forgave you, so also do ye (Colossians 3:13).*

**I should forgive because my survival demands forgiveness and my future requires it.** Forgiveness doesn't erase the past, but it surely changes the future. It is impossible to have a peaceful future while harboring unforgiveness in your heart. Without forgiveness, life is governed by an endless cycle of sorrow, loss and resentment. It is only when we forgive that we are forgiven.

*After this manner therefore pray ye: Our Father which art in heaven, Hallowed be thy name. [10] Thy kingdom come, Thy will be done in earth, as it is in heaven. [11] Give us this day our daily bread. [12]And forgive us our debts, as we forgive our debtors. [13]And lead us not into temptation, but deliver us from evil: For thine is the kingdom, and the power, and the glory, for ever. Amen (Matthew 6:9-13).*

Most people know the Lord's Prayer and usually stop reading it, or saying it, at the Amen at the end of verse

13, but the next two verses are every bit as much a part of Jesus' instructions to us.

*For if ye forgive men their trespasses, your heavenly Father will also forgive you: [15] but if ye forgive not men their trespasses, neither will your Father forgive your trespasses (Matthew 6:14-15).*

This is not the only time that Jesus made forgiving others a condition of being forgiven of our own sin.

*And when ye stand praying, forgive, if ye have ought against any: that your Father also which is in heaven may forgive you your trespasses. [26] But if ye do not forgive, neither will your Father which is in heaven forgive your trespasses (Mark 11:25-26).*

*"And when ye stand praying..."* That phrase certainly indicates that forgiveness is a condition for receiving answers to our prayers. We close another door when we hold unforgiveness in our heart. God doesn't forgive us of our sins and our prayers are not answered. Jesus made it clear that when we are right with God, we will be right with others. On the other hand, if we are not right with others, we will not be right with God. That's a very strong motive for forgiving others. We want to have a healthy, flourishing relationship with God.

If we ask God to forgive us, it is only righteous and just for us to grant forgiveness to others.

"I firmly believe a great many prayers are not answered because we are not willing to forgive someone." ~Dwight L. Moody~

Once we understand what God in Christ did for us, refusing to forgive those who have wronged us is to be like the wicked, ungrateful, unjust servant according to Matthew 18:23-35.

*Therefore, is the kingdom of heaven likened unto a certain king, which would take account of his servants. [24] And when he had begun to reckon, one was brought unto him, which owed him ten thousand talents. [25] But forasmuch as he had not to pay, his lord commanded him to be sold, and his wife, and children, and all that he had, and payment to be made. [26] The servant therefore fell down, and worshipped him, saying, Lord, have patience with me, and I will pay thee all. [27] Then the lord of that servant was moved with compassion, and loosed him, and forgave him the debt. [28] But the same servant went out, and found one of his fellow servants, which owed him an hundred pence: and he laid hands on him, and took him by the throat, saying, Pay me that thou owest. [29] And his fellow servant fell down at his feet, and besought him, saying, Have patience with me, and I will pay thee all. [30] And he would not: but went and cast him into prison, till he should pay the debt. [31] So when his fellow servants saw what was done, they were very sorry, and came and told unto their lord all that was done. [32] Then his lord, after that he had called him, said unto him, O thou wicked servant, I forgave thee all that debt, because thou desiredst me: [33] shouldest not thou also have had compassion on thy fellow servant, even as I had pity on thee? [34] And his lord was wroth, and delivered him to the tormentors, till he should pay all that was due unto him. [35] So likewise shall my heavenly Father do also unto you, if ye from your hearts forgive not every one his brother their trespasses.*

This parable shows us that unforgiveness turns us over to the torturers. There are a lot of torturers in the earth today; sickness, fear, addiction, mental illness, poverty, bondage, stress, anxiety and multitudes more.

Forgiveness is not always easy. Sometimes it feels more painful than the wound we suffered and yet, there is no release of our own suffering without forgiveness. In my experience, I have never seen one truly recover from an injury inflicted upon them by another until they forgive.

"Forgiveness doesn't make the other person right; it makes you free." ~Stormie Omartian~

## How Does Forgiveness Work?

I encourage you to lay aside everything you have heard or assumed about forgiveness and let a single word impress itself on your mind: the word is "release." Don't make it any more complicated than that; release. To forgive means to choose to take someone whom you have been holding in your debt, whether justly, or unjustly, and releasing him or her of any obligation due to you.

Forgiving Ray did not say that what he did was okay. It is not turning a blinded eye towards injustice. Forgiving him simply means that I chose to release him from any personal accountability to me. He still had natural consequences to face and He had to answer to God, but I released him from having to answer to me.

When we forgive, we release the other person so God can do what only He can do. It's only when we choose to forgive and let go that God can then take over. As long as we hold onto an offense God doesn't get involved in our healing. It is only when we trust Him and choose to forgive that He will take the heartache and pain and work on our behalf to rebuild our lives.

The first thing we must do when we think we should forgive someone who has wronged us is to make sure that our actions rise to the level of true forgiveness.

*To whom ye forgive anything, I forgive also: for if I forgave anything, to whom I forgave it, for your sakes forgave I it in the person of Christ (2 Corinthians 2:10).*

When it comes to forgiving, here is what the Lord requires; Forgive as the Lord forgave you." How do you do that? You let go. You choose to release the offender and turn to God for grace to do the rest.

The prophet Micah tells us why God forgives.

*Who is a God like you, who pardons sin and forgives the transgression of the remnant of his inheritance? You do not stay angry forever but delight to show mercy (Micah 7:18).*

God forgives because He delights in showing mercy. Mercy is God's "thing." It's what brings Him pleasure. He forgives quickly, and often. It's amazing that God delights to forgive because He has more to forgive than anyone. Every human God has ever created has sinned against Him, usually many times every day, yet He still delights to forgive. In forgiving we bring God pleasure by extending mercy to the guilty party. When we truly forgive, we release mercy to the offender and we release it to ourselves as well.

In Matthew 18, Jesus' disciple Peter asked Jesus, "How many times shall I forgive my brother when he sins against me? Up to seven times?" Jesus answered with a parable in which a man owed a king 10,000 talents, probably equivalent to hundreds of thousands of dollars today. The man was on the verge of being sold into slavery, along with his wife and children to pay the debt. He pleaded with the king for mercy and the king generously cancelled his debt. This was an act of forgiveness and release.

In Jeremiah's prophecy about the new covenant, God says,

*I will forgive their wickedness and will remember their sins no more (Jeremiah 31:34).*

It's not that God becomes unaware of what has happened. God does not remember our sins in the sense that He doesn't hold them against us. Again, it's forgiveness and release. If you have ever been concerned that you haven't forgiven because you haven't forgotten, remember that forgiving simply means release.

*Whose soever sins ye remit, they are remitted unto them; and whose soever sins ye retain, they are retained (John 20:23).*

This verse has been fiercely debated for centuries and I don't want to jump into that ring. I would simply like to state what I believe to be the most obvious lesson Jesus is teaching here. Sin can bring eternal destruction, but it also brings present destruction. Sin destroys people emotionally and physically in this life, too. I believe it is the present destruction that sin brings into people's lives that Jesus gave us power to remit.

If you still harbor thoughts of malice or discontent against another, you may have spoken words of forgiveness, but the forgiveness isn't genuine because mercy isn't present. When we truly forgive, we will feel released, as well. That may take a little time, but the decision to forgive sets us on the right path and we can fully expect that release to come. You will know when your heart is clear because the memory of the offense will no longer have the sting of death. It will simply be a memory and have no power to cripple you.

Jesus sets the high standard of kingdom living and we need to follow His example. We also need to strive for grace. We can, and should, freely give away the grace we've been given.

*But love ye your enemies, and do good, and lend, hoping for nothing again; and your reward shall be great, and ye shall be the children of the Highest: for he is kind unto the unthankful and to the evil. 36 Be ye therefore merciful, as your Father also is merciful. 37 Judge not, and ye shall not be judged: condemn not, and ye shall not be condemned: forgive, and ye shall be forgiven (Luke 6:35-37).*

Being willing to forgive is not a reluctant act of obedience to God. It is being merciful to the undeserving and that happens only when God's character become life in our wicked and hardened hearts.

# CHAPTER EIGHTEEN

# The Answer to ALL

As Ray and I minister together I am humbled at how God uses our story to set people free from years of unforgiveness. Numerous times people have told me that when they compare their problems to ours, they see how insignificant their matter is and have been able to forgive and release their offender. I watch with joy as God comes and delivers them from hatred and bitterness that had tormented them and robbed them of peace.

I met a woman whose son had been murdered eighteen years earlier. I had such compassion for her because all those many years later she was still trapped in unending grief, unable to forgive the one who had taken his life. I could tell from other things said in our conversation that she was in her late forties but she looked to be at least thirty years older than that. Her brow was deeply furrowed and her face was etched with sadness. Unforgiveness had ambushed her and stolen her youth. Thankfully, it was not too late for Jesus to deliver her and for the Holy Spirit to fill her heart with peace.

Perhaps you are like that woman and have been harboring unforgiveness for years. Forgiveness couldn't change her past, but it could definitely change her future, and it can do the same for you. You may not have visible, outward signs of deterioration like she did, but I can assure you that if you refuse to forgive, you are rotting on the inside. Unforgiveness is a heartless taskmaster and it will consume and destroy you. I encourage you to ask our gracious and loving heavenly Father to forgive you for disobeying His commandment to forgive, and to give you grace to do everything He wants you to do. Please pray this prayer from your heart.

Dear Heavenly Father, in the name of Your Son, Jesus, I ask You to forgive me for refusing to forgive. By faith in You and Your grace I choose to forgive everyone who has hurt me. Help me set [name anyone who has offended you] free and release them to You. I choose to forgive them, just as You have forgiven me, and I ask for Your grace and power to never agree with unforgiveness and bitterness again. Amen.

If that was a genuine heartfelt prayer, the Lord will be quick to answer it and will begin immediately to release the hurt and relieve the pain you've been suffering. He can change your living hell into a gift. Receive that gift by faith.

On the day God asked me to do what was humanly impossible, I simply agreed with Him. I simply said 'yes' and from that day forward I have set my heart to agree with Him over and over again. I have never had a moment of regret for following Him, and neither will you. Agree with God. Agree and follow. ***THAT, my friend, is the answer to ALL.***

## Fire Up Your Power Tools:
### A Practical Handbook for Using the Gift of Tongues
**Linda Markowitz**

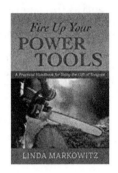

What happens when you pray in tongues? Jesus taught us to pray to the Father, "Thy Kingdom come; Thy will be done in earth, as it is in heaven." Thankfully, Jesus did not leave us to figure out how to do that on our own; He sent us great help. With the empowering of the Holy Spirit all Christians live in a fully equipped "smart house"; but the miraculous and unlimited resources of heaven cannot benefit us until we know how to interact with the Holy Spirit and engage His power. If you want to see God's covenant promises tangibly manifest in your life, you will find this book to be an indispensable tool. In it you will learn how to co-labor with the Holy Spirit to make the abundant life a reality for you.

Find both of Linda's books at **Amazon.com**